"I love this book because you can [...]
Connors offers you positive and pr[...]
schools and classrooms all over the [...]
even more exciting, engaging, caring[...]
tors who love their students and yearn [...]
happy and meaningful relationships [...] schools were the
bedrock of raising student achievement. It is the perfect sequel to Neila
Connors's first book, *If You Don't Feed the Teachers, They'll Eat the Students,* a
book that I continue to share with teachers I work with and is beloved by all."

Judith Enright, Education Consultant

"*If You Don't F.E.E.D. the Students, They S.T.A.R.V.E.* is filled with a menu of
strategies, supports, activities and ideas to challenge our students, ourselves,
and our schools to be the best we can be!"

Anna M. Farrell, Retired Educator

"Dr. Connors's newest buffet of positive strategies in education today is a
must-read. Sample her ideas about making learning relevant for students.
Celebrate her personal recipe box of changes you can make in your
students. Going to school should be a 5-star experience for our kids. Stir it
up. Spice it up. Get ready to be waited on by the finest education chef herself."

Patty Dailey, Middle School Teacher

"In my 40 years in education, never has a book been so critical. This book
reinforces our *why* and shows us how we can transform schools through
humor and knowledge. Every staff member will find renewal and discovery
through this extraordinary collection of strategies."

Martinrex Kedziora, Ed.D., Superintendent,
. Moreno Valley Unified School District

"I have used Dr. Connors's work with my graduate-level students, in
Educational Leadership courses, for the past several years. These educators
are hungry for more of Neila's positive strategies and excellent ideas.
Dr. Connors's newest book, *If You Don't F.E.E.D. the Students, They S.T.A.R.V.E.*
provides a delectable menu of choices for practitioners of all experience
levels. Please reserve me a table for 25."

Glady Van Harpen, PhD, University of Wisconsin Oshkosh

If You Don't F.E.E.D. the Students, They S.T.A.R.V.E.

If You Don't F.E.E.D. the Students, They S.T.A.R.V.E.

Neila A. Connors, PhD

JB JOSSEY-BASS™
A Wiley Brand

Jossey-Bass books and products are available through most bookstores. To contact Jossey-Bass directly call our Customer Care Department within the U.S. at 800-956-7739, outside the U.S. at 317-572-3986, or fax 317-572-4002.

Wiley also publishes its books in a variety of electronic formats and by print-on-demand. For more information about Wiley products, visit www.wiley.com.

Library of Congress Cataloging-in-Publication Data is Available:

ISBN 9780470577790 (paperback)
ISBN 9781118418383 (ePDF)
ISBN 9781118415368 (ePub)

Cover Design and Illustrations: Paul McCarthy

Printed in the United States of America
FIRST EDITION
PB Printing V10016733_010620

This book is dedicated most importantly to Helen Irene Mooney Connors, my best friend, mentor, and mother, who was my most talented teacher of all (I miss and love you every day). As I look back at all of the basics and learnings she taught me, I am amazed how much ahead of her time she lived. She was the mother extraordinaire, filled with so much love, excitement, and compassion that she authentically lived every day to the fullest, smiling and laughing her way through life.

It is also dedicated to my three favorite teachers: Mrs. Charlotte Pignatelli (2nd grade), Mrs. Mae Brown (high school home economics), and Mr. Stephen Sable (high school psychology) – each inspired me to pursue teaching and be the best possible in life – and to all of the other extraordinary teachers in the world.

And to my favorite principal: Mr. Paul Perachi (Lenox Memorial High School, Lenox, Massachusetts), who wrote to me, "One thing I learned, early on, when working with kids was that you needed to be honest and straightforward in all of your dealings. Kids can smell a phony from a mile away and they respect your honesty even if they don't agree with you or like what you are saying or doing. You've obviously had a distinguished career, and I am honored to have been a little part of it."

BRIEF CONTENTS

CONTENTS

7 Communication: Succinct, Effective, and Ongoing,   103

8 Satisfaction: We Left F.E.D. and Eager to Return,   119

9 Comment Card: The Opportunity to Provide Feedback,   131

10 Fun: An Environment That Everyone Enjoys,   141

11 "Check, Please": Reflection Shows the Experience Was Worth It,   151

ACKNOWLEDGMENTS

I further acknowledge the following people who have inspired, loved, and supported me throughout this adventure:

- My dearest friends who all pushed me along to complete this project and birth this baby:
  - Dr. John Lounsbury – my friend, my mentor, my hero.
  - Dr. James and Debbie Crosier – always my biggest cheerleaders and amazing friends.
  - Jeanette Phillips – my "sister" who puts up with my right-brained lifestyle as she lives her left-brained and one of the most student-oriented, remarkable principals I ever worked with.
  - Dr. Martinrex Kedziora – who also continuously asked how much I had completed and when would it be published and for being the Superintendent Extraordinaire at the Moreno Unified School District.
  - Judy Sanders Enright – the most organized person I ever knew, who brings out the best in everyone and gets things done.
  - Dr. Glady Van Harpen – even though she lives in the coldest part of our country, she is the warmest and kindest person in the world.
  - Dr. Richard Ramsey – who is always checking on me and bringing me back to reality – thanks, Rev.
  - Kathy Shewey – the most caring listener, who is always there for anyone who needs a shoulder or a room for the night.
  - Cathy Egley – one of the best principals I have ever worked with, who loves students and gives her "all" in everything she does.
- My St. Leo College/University divas/besties. We met in 1971 fresh out of high school and are still in touch and acting like we are still in college:
  - Patty Kinney Dailey
  - Anna Farrell

- • Janelle Buck Walkley
- • Joan D. Petrie
- My Thomasville City Schools, Thomasville, Georgia, team. You are remarkable and make my day every day. Thank you:
  - • My students – I LOVE EACH and EVERY ONE OF YOU.
  - • Mrs. Gwen Scott-Morrow
  - • Mrs. Tina McBride
  - • Mrs. Carla DuBose
  - • Mr. Neal Ford
  - • Mrs. Katie McCloud
  - • Mrs. Kimsey Hodge
  - • Dr. Tret Witherspoon
  - • Mrs. Pam Cloud
  - • Mr. Espy
- My Thomas University, Thomasville, Georgia, colleagues who gave me the opportunity to get back into the classroom through the GEAR UP program:
  - • Ms. Melanie Martin
  - • Mr. Leon Smith
  - • Mr. Kendrick Duncan
  - • Ms. Vera Clark
  - • Mr. Deandre Robinson
  - • Mrs. Teresa Treat
- And last but not least, to Bradley Craig Buysse, my best friend, partner, and soul mate, who put up with chaos and a total mass of papers everywhere as I wrote, who supported my efforts, and blissfully cheered my completion. Love you!

ABOUT THE AUTHOR

Dr. Neila A. Connors is the founder and president of N.A.C. (Networking And Client) CONNECTIONS INC., a corporation dedicated to the implementation of *positive attitudes and actions* in people. Her primary focus is to coach people on how to "build their own bridge for a successful life." Her philosophy is based on Napoleon Hill's quote: "If you can conceive it and believe it, you can achieve it."

Presently, Neila works for Thomasville University in Thomasville, Georgia, as a site coordinator for the GEAR UP program, which places her in MacIntyre Park Middle School teaching 6th, 7th, and 8th grade math. She loves being in the classroom.

Throughout her career, Neila has had the privilege of working with students in grades K–12. She has been an elementary teacher, a middle school teacher, and an administrator. She also was an online adjunct professor online at Florida State University for four years.

Previously, Neila worked at the Florida Department of Education, responsible for coordinating the development of the middle and high school state curriculum frameworks, working with high school teachers and administrators throughout the state. She also was the director of Middle Grades and later was responsible for the state International Baccalaureate and Advanced Placement programs. She also served as a tenured professor in the Department of Middle and Secondary Education at Valdosta State University, Valdosta, Georgia.

Her research has been in the areas of teacher advisory programs, successful counselors, attitudes of students from rural areas, positive teachers and their characteristics, and homework. Among her most notable publications are *S.O.S. (Success-Oriented Strategies) for Teachers of At-Risk Early Adolescents: P.S. – All Early Adolescents Are at Risk!* and *Homework: A New Direction.* Her most recent publication, *If You Don't Feed the Teachers, They Eat the Students,* a guide for all educators, has received many enthusiastic reviews.

Neila has written numerous articles. She has presented to public and private school educators, school boards, superintendents, state and national organizations, parents, counselors, international school educators, and corporations in the 50 states, Canada, and Europe.

Born in Lenox Dale, Massachusetts, Neila received her bachelor's degree from St. Leo College in Florida and her master's and doctorate degrees from Florida State University, Tallahassee, Florida. She is proud to be a die-hard Florida State Seminole and introduces herself as A BELIEVER IN PEOPLE AND A LOVER OF LIFE!

These are very interesting and challenging times in education. With the emphasis on the Common Core State Standards (CCSS), Georgia Milestones, teacher assessment, and high-stakes testing, on top of many other new practices and programs, many feel inundated and overly stressed. Plates are full and anxiety is high in classrooms and schools everywhere. Veteran teachers are asking why, while new teachers are asking how.

There are too many cooks in the kitchen deciding what is best for our students and the progression of education. Everyone is screaming accountability, assessment, accreditation, authenticity, and adaptability as our students and teachers are just trying to endure. And while our standards increase and our testing toughens, the real world just uses a search engine to find information at a moment's notice.

Think about it. In this day and age, if we are dining with a friend or colleague and they mention a topic, term, or philosophy that we are unfamiliar with – what do we do? In less than two minutes, we have a complete description and a base foundation from searching on our phone. Yet our schools are still in the antiquated mode of the "drill and kill," "death by ditto," and the "sage on the stage" methods. The tests get more difficult, the teachers are overwhelmed, and students are looking for alternatives via online and virtual learning because there is too much to learn that never will be applied in the real world. So unfortunate, especially when the extraordinary teachers have the answers.

The foremost objective for writing this book is to focus on what really matters and remind everyone to NEVER lose sight of what is important – relationships, relevance, recognition, and connections with our students. If students don't feel that the adults they are working with truly care – learning does not occur. That is the reality. We cannot tolerate new trends mandated by elected officials with inflated egos to take away from doing whatever it takes to F.E.E.D (Fuel, Engage, Empower Daily) students on a regular basis so they do not S.T.A.R.V.E. (Stop Trying And Reject Valuable Education). Students and their overall welfare must be our major concentration. My dream is that everyone working in the best profession ever – education – will take the time to connect with students through positive attitudes, open communication, active participation, commitment, and recognition.

Additionally, I believe that repetition is the mother of skill. Therefore, you will see important activities and ideas shared numerous times throughout the chapters. I believe when you first learn something you accept it (hopefully), when you hear it again you believe it (conditionally), and when it is shared a third or fourth time you actually put it into practice (end goal). My aspiration is that after devouring this cookbook, you will find many takeaways that you will put into practice and begin formulating your own methods to F.E.E.D. students.

The following chapters will provide the recipes to authentically and realistically accomplish what is most important. This will ensure our students do not S.T.A.R.V.E. and bona fide, reality-based learning will occur. This book is designed in a "cookbook" fashion so you can easily move from section to section and not have to digest everything in order.

INTRODUCTION

Welcome to your personal "dining" opportunity. It is my pleasure to share my views and thinking with you. The purpose of this book is to validate that like a fine "five-star restaurant" and extraordinary dining experience, a fine educational experience can produce a state of reverence and satisfaction and be quite tasty and fulfilling, nutritious and delicious; which is why teachers who F.E.E.D (Fuel, Engage, Empower Daily) their students ensure that students do not S.T.A.R.V.E. (Stop Trying And Reject Valuable Education) My former book *If You Don't Feed the Teachers, They Eat the Students!* focused primarily on "feeding" principals, assistant/vice principals, administrative teams, and teachers.

This book will take you on an excursion "from soup to nuts," covering what I believe is imperative to F.E.E.D. students the best education possible at ALL grade levels from all backgrounds and diverse conditions. The concentration will be on improving attitudes and achievement by developing and sustaining positive relationships through open communication, active participation, commitment, and recognition. The goal will be to assist schools and educators in moving from *ordinary* to *extraordinary*.

Going from ordinary to extraordinary means we really need to look at our educational system constructively. Truthfully, everyone wants schools to be better, but the reality is that no one wants them to be different. My friend and mentor, Dr. John Lounsbury, would always share that if Rip van Winkle were to wake up today after 100 years of sleeping, he would not know how to drive a car, use a cell phone, turn on a TV, or get money from an ATM, but he would feel comfortable in our schools because many have not changed much – kids in desks, in rows, teacher in the front (yes, with new technology but doing the same thing) and the "sage on the stage" with little time for interaction, reaction, discussion, questions, or reflection.

Extraordinary is when top-chef teachers use distinctive and various teaching strategies to include all learning styles through interdisciplinary instruction. Extraordinary people make a commitment, go above and beyond, get things done, inspire, create, and serve. Purchase the book *The Fred Factor: Every Person's Guide to Making the Ordinary Extraordinary* by Mark Sanborn for all staff members and discuss it during a staff meeting.

My Style

My style is definitely for all of my fellow right-brainers. However, I have forced my left-brain to function for the folks who truly run the world. If you are not sure what side of your brain is dominant, here is a simple assessment: Left-brainers have FILES, right-brainers have PILES, and no-brainers have PILES of FILES. Consequently, in this "cookbook/guide to success" there is something for everyone: all grade levels, all teachers, and all administrators to F.E.E.D. students.

Dispersed throughout, you will find many notes, suggestions, observations, and dreams I have chronicled throughout my career. Whenever I attend a meeting, conference, or staff development session I take notes in my journal. Additionally, many thoughts and ideas come to mind at different times that I journal. I always try to give credit where credit is due if possible and apologize in advance if an idea appears to be without acknowledgment. You will also find a lot of quotes. Attempts have been made to attach the correct person to the quote, but over time, some quotes become attributed to the wrong source. As Abraham Lincoln said, "Not everything you read on the Internet is true." Finally, for all of you "acronym-a-holics" like me, you will LOVE this book. So, sit back, relax, and enjoy. We aim to please. As you dine, we hope you will find an array of appetizers, meals, desserts, and recipes to suit your needs.

What Do You Expect from a Five-Star Restaurant, and How Does That Translate to a Five-Star School?

When you make plans to go to a five-star restaurant, you have certain expectations. Your foremost desire is that the focus be on *you*, the CUSTOMER.

If you have had a great dining experience, you should be able to answer yes to the following questions:

- ✓ Did I feel genuinely welcomed?
- ✓ Was the facility clean and comfortable with a friendly and safe atmosphere?
- ✓ Was the experience fabulous/extraordinary?
- ✓ Was there someone who made it extra special?
- ✓ Will I share this experience with others?
- ✓ Did I leave satiated and F.E.D.?
- ✓ Am I looking forward to returning?

The same questions can be asked of students when assessing the success of a five-star school. We will address each question thoroughly in future chapters.

My recent encounter with a five-star restaurant was in the Denver Tech Center in Colorado at a restaurant named Del Frisco's Double Eagle Steakhouse. The evening was in celebration of a dear friend's birthday. Her husband, son, and daughter-in law joined us. Obviously, the company was the foundation for a fabulous evening, but we also had HIGH expectations for the restaurant, which were met and beyond.

With that aside, as I reflect on the specific components or ingredients that made this event so extraordinary and noteworthy, I easily concluded that Del Frisco's Steakhouse provided us with a significant and noteworthy experience.

> If you can experience all or at least most of the components from a FIVE STAR RESTAURANT, you will feel the money and time spent was worth it. Similarly, we want our students to feel F.E.D. (F-ulfilled, E-nergized, and De-stressed) upon departing from school every day. Our priority is to strive to meet that purpose.

The following chapters/experiences will identify each component and penetrate more deeply into the elements listed, providing the ingredients to make it happen. Understandably, an entire book can be written on each topic, but here you will be given the nuggets to entice and stimulate your pallet. Accordingly, I will attempt to provide a "buffet" of recommendations for you to select from to F.E.E.D. the students in your school, remembering that students are the *customers* and deserve thoughtful treatment on a daily basis. Our *ultimate* goal is to Fuel, Engage, and Empower Daily (F.E.E.D) so everyone leaves Fullfilled, Energized, and Destressed (F.E.D) and so students do not S.T.A.R.V.E. – Stop Trying And Reject Valuable Education.

Sit back, relax, and relish your experience. *Bon appétit!*

CHAPTER 1

"Welcome!": A Courteous Greeting, and Everyone Is Valued

Everyone Is Treated with Dignity and Respect

Patrons want to feel important when going to a *five-star restaurant*. Upon their arrival, they are treated with dignity and respect and feel valued. A *five-star school* (FSS) does the same to students, teachers, parents, and anyone who enters. And in *five-star schools* where we F.E.E.D. (Fuel, Engage, Empower Daily), everything is transparent as well. First impressions are predominant. From the minute students, parents, and community members arrive at the school, they are greeted with an array of messages affirming "Welcome to OUR school!" The *appearance* of the building mirrors the respect *for* the people who work and learn there and *from* the people responsible for its existence.

Signs of a student-focused school begin with the outside appearance. Have you ever driven to an unknown restaurant recommended by a friend and, upon arrival, departed without even entering because of how it looked on the outside? Unfortunately, our students can't leave. Therefore, it is our responsibility to ensure that the grounds are neat, groomed, and inviting (William Perky). Getting students involved in the upkeep of the school is an excellent way to have students "own" their school.

Greet and treat others with *dignity* and *respect*. What does that really imply? Let's look at dignity first.

Dignity

The dictionary definition of dignity reads, "The quality or state of being worthy of self-esteem and self-respect." Dignity is one of those words like tolerance, love, and compassion that we all instinctively believe is necessary for success but we all have different interpretations of how to show it. If we asked 10 people to define dignity and give tangible activities that demonstrate it,

> Even if the student's life away from school is bleak and miserable, she/he will work if what she/he finds in school is satisfying.
>
> **William Glasser**

we would have 10 different ideas and models. While dignity is difficult to delineate, we all can clearly articulate when we have NOT been treated with dignity. Dignity, in my opinion, means appreciating others as they are and treating them as THEY want to be treated.

Some suggestions for teachers to discuss about creating an atmosphere of dignity are:

❖ Articulate and model a policy to prevent any form of prejudice, abuse, and bullying.

❖ Emphasize dignity in every activity, ritual, and schoolwide event.

❖ Treat every person that enters your building respectfully (ensure there is a process to know *who* is entering your building).

❖ LISTEN to and support others, allowing everyone to express their opinions and beliefs in a safe and nurturing environment.

❖ Provide techniques and solutions to identify those with low self-esteem issues and needing positive reinforcement.

❖ Emphasize the self-worth of others by providing as many positive activities and choices as possible.

❖ Provide a process for anyone feeling bullied or unsafe and communicate it to all.

❖ Do whatever it takes to create a RESPECTFUL environment for all.

Now that we have defined dignity, what is respect? The dictionary reads, "To feel or show deferential regard for, esteem, to avoid violation of or interference with, a feeling of appreciation, the state of being regarded with honor or esteem." Again, we could ask the same 10 people to define respect and give specific examples of *respectful* schools. To have fabulous *communication*, we must have *respect*. We must be cognizant of culture to understand respect.

Respect

Respect is more easily demonstrated through actions, words, programs, rituals, policies, and activities. Respect covers a vast amount of components including:

• Ourselves

• Others (looks, actions, and personalities)

- The environment
- Physical space
- Different viewpoints, philosophies, beliefs, and opinions
- Religion
- Diversity
- Gender
- Lifestyle choices
- Ethnic origin
- Physical and mental ability

FSSs recognize these components and have rich conversations about what happens in the building to provide respect to all.

My dear friend Gene Bedley, the executive director for the National Character Education Center, is the master of teaching respect. He has an entire program on ensuring your school teaches and models respect. Gene has eight *rules of respect*:

1. Everyone has dignity and worth. Human beings are valuable and unique. Each person is an unrepeatable miracle woven together like no other person.

2. Acknowledge and validate others' feelings and ideas. Kindness is the language the deaf can hear and the blind can see.

3. Focused eye contact and the ability to repeat what others share will demonstrate active listening. The first step to effective listening is to *stop* talking.

4. When exchanging ideas with another person, seek first to understand by asking clarifying questions.

5. Recognize that your body language communicates as much as your words. Your actions speak so loudly, people can't hear you.

6. Recognize that every person has something to teach. To teach is to learn; to listen is to learn more.

7. The way you treat others is proof of the respect you have for yourself.

8. Express generosity and kindness to those in need. Love *never* fails.

Gene's program recommends that schools begin a Respect Campaign focusing on "IT'S NOT COOL TO BE CRUEL." He emphasizes to treat others with respect and encourages everyone to wear buttons that ask, "Do you know what I like about you?" to also spark intense discussions.

> **"**
> What comes from a person when they are "squeezed" shows what's inside.
> **Wayne Dyer**
> **"**

Realistically, we all know that dignity and respect begin at home. However, we cannot put our heads in the sand and ignore the fact that some students arrive at our doors with no understanding of what it means to promote dignity and respect. We must deal with this issue head on to create our FSS.

A perfect example of this was in my first year of teaching. I was from Massachusetts teaching in an extremely southern school, Lacoochee Elementary in Lacoochee, Florida. As a young, single teacher from the North, I was amazed at how the students would always respond, "yes ma'am" or "no ma'am" when asked a question. I "disrespectfully" asked them not to call me "ma'am" because I did NOT understand the culture and associated *ma'am* with age. Immediately, my wonderful principal called me into his office and politely, with dignity and respect, taught me that it was the southern culture to refer to adults as ma'am and sir. I learned a valuable lesson that day. I also personally learned to use the terms *ma'am* and *sir* with pride. Teachers must respect others' cultures and learn as much about the culture as possible.

I believe there is a hierarchy occurring when we concentrate initially on respect. *Respectful* adults then focus on *relationships,* which leads to *relevance* in the school and classroom. Creating an environment of care and compassion is based on relationships – *all* relationships. This is a school where a priority is placed on fostering meaningful student-to-student, student-to-adults, adults-to-students, and adult-to-adult relationships. This is a school where bullying, racial comments, and inappropriate behavior are absolutely unacceptable. This is an FSS where adults and students enjoy and look forward to long-term positive relationships.

Relationships

Marzano states, "Positive relationships mean less work engaging students, easier classroom management, a longer focus time, and students willing to take risks." Teachers must build these relationships through communication, seeing students as worthy and responsible, keeping commitments, being *kind*, clarifying expectations, and being loyal, fair, and consistent. Some simple ways to build relationships include:

➤ Be waiting at your door when students arrive. You can assess any problems, the happy kids, and other emotions about to enter your classroom.

➤ Be aware of who you call on throughout the lesson. Try to develop a culture where every student feels comfortable to share.

➤ Respect, respect, respect – all students until they don't earn it. Then attempt to establish a one-on-one where the topic is discussed.

➢ Make sure you work on consistency. Students pick up on inconsistencies immediately. In some schools, the only consistency is inconsistency.

➢ Have a "bell ringer" or "do now" activity on the board that students must start on immediately upon entering the classroom. All of the teachers at MacIntryre Park Middle School (MPMS) practice this strategy and praise students who follow the instructions.

➢ Teach students what your expectations are and *what they look like*. Go over them daily during the first month of school. And occasionally when a review is needed, start over again. Do NOT assume students know what you mean when you say, "Enter the room quietly." To *teach* the student, you must *reach* the student.

Building relationships is a precondition to student learning. Students recognize the adults who do not enjoy their job, the students, and ultimately their life and can detect a phony in a heartbeat. It takes very special people to teach and be in education. No matter what your job title or classification is:

> Superintendent, district level staff, principal, assistant/vice principal, support staff, – we ALL are TEACHERS first because students observe and note EVERYTHING we *do, say,* and *model.*

No matter what grade level, students recognize when adults enjoy being around them. There is an old saying I first heard in undergraduate school, "Students don't care how much we know until they know how much we care." My friend and colleague, Dr. Richard Ramsey, always says in his presentations "You know the teachers and adults that students love; students are always hanging around their classroom/office and look forward to seeing the adult. If there are no students at your door during the day, they just don't like you."

Jeanette Phillips, a former middle school principal in Fresno, California, shared this story: One day she was standing in the hallway talking and laughing with two seventh grade girls. A female teacher, known to all to be a "lemon sandwich eater" (grouchy and unhappy) and not student-friendly, walked up to Jeanette and the girls and sarcastically remarked, "Don't you just *love* these students?" to which one of the seventh grade girls responded, "If you love the students so much, why doesn't your face ever show it?" Wow! As my mother, Helen, always said, "The proof is in the pudding."

We begin with *respect*, which fosters positive *relationships* that lead to *relevance*. Creating a relevant atmosphere of *care* and *compassion* is vital.

Care and Compassion

Compassion makes the world a better place. People who are compassionate do anything possible to help others; they are just kind. Compassionate teachers emphasize to students that their behavior can change the entire climate of the school. These students take pride in serving others, showing others that they truly care, teaching others how to be empathetic, recognizing others' gifts and talents, and understanding their feelings.

Teachers take the time to get to know their students and authentically *listen*, which will be addressed throughout because it is so important. As Mark Twain said, "If we were to speak more than listen, we would have been given two mouths instead of two ears." Furthermore, they continually ask students for feedback. It is amazing how the smallest caring gesture can make a major difference and have a huge effect on the students.

Gene Bedley, director for the National Character Education Center in a session titled "Touch the Heart, Change the Student" through Rachel's Challenge (www.rachelschallenge.org), explains that in schools where adults model care and compassion as well as teaching it to students, success follows. We know that caring is a skill that can be learned, and people who care are surrounded by a contagious energy that is inviting to others. They are genuine; they go above and beyond.

> **"**
> Caring is a skill. The beaver is very skilled at its craft. It knows exactly what to do to fix a dam. The last thing a beaver needs is someone on the bank shouting out dam instructions.
> **(author unknown)**
> **"**

Wellness

An organization that promotes "wellness" recognizes the utmost importance of taking care of people in body, mind, and spirit. Wellness is showing up and being in the moment. Wellness initiatives are evident in all healthy organizations, but especially schools. Five-star restaurants provide for their employees and customers wellness by serving high-quality food in a fine setting. Five-star schools emphasize to students, teachers, parents, and the community the importance of taking care of oneself and each other. A healthy school is a happy school, creating an emphasis on wellness of all.

Wellness encompasses the staff as well as the students. Schoolwide wellness matters are addressed regularly because they augment learning and life. In a climate where staff wellness is imperative:

- Less absenteeism occurs.
- Productivity increases.
- Morale increases.
- Future employees want to work there.
- The school's image is positive in the community.
- There is less turnover.
- Healthy behaviors are modeled.
- Adults are healthy role models for students.
- Adults enjoy each other, students, and their profession.
- Ongoing health screenings are available.
- Professional development is crucial and ongoing.
- The district personnel applaud and support school wellness initiatives.

In a environment of where student wellness is imperative:

- Students learn to make healthy choices.
- Health and physical education classes are viewed as a vitally important component of the school curriculum.
- Counseling services are available for students who deal with health problems.
- Every student has an adult/mentor in the school who is an advocate and coach.
- Life skills classes teach students how to live a healthy and productive life.
- Adults recognize that health and success are related.
- The loss of physical education or fine arts classes is never used as a disciplinary consequence.

- The school lunch program initiates and supports healthy dining and includes a breakfast program for students who may not receive breakfast at home.

- "Shake breaks" or recess are a part of the school activities.

- Students are encouraged to bring healthy snacks and food to school.

- Healthy living styles are modeled and discussed through the entire year.

- Students participate in community service projects to further healthy living.

- The promotion of wellness extends into the homes and community.

- Sound fitness programs are available for all via intramurals and physical education.

- Every student is encouraged to participate in extracurricular activities (sports, music, drama, clubs).

- The dining area supports cleanliness and a healthy, pleasant atmosphere.

A fine dining experience includes "positiveness," where everyone from the maître d to the servers to the busboys have a positive attitude about what they do. Positiveness must also exist in a FSS. We all know that the foundation to being positive is *attitude*. A positive attitude is the most important quality adults must possess to F.E.E.D. students so they don't S.T.A.R.V.E. (Stop Trying And Reject Valuable Education). Students know the adults who love being at the school and those who do not. Life is a choice, and every one of us chooses our attitude every day. When adults elect to work in schools with students they must make that *choice* because they like students, they believe they can make a difference, and they will do whatever it takes to help students achieve; consistency.

The longer I live, the more I realize the effect of attitude on life. Attitude is more important than the past, education, money, circumstances, than failures or successes, than what other people think or say or do. It is more critical than appearance, giftedness, or skill. It will make or break a school, company, church, or home. The significant attribute is that we have a choice each day to choose our attitude and hug and embrace it for the day. We can't change the past or the fact that people act a certain way. We can't change the inevitable. The only thing we can do is play on the one string we have left, and that is our *attitude*. Life is 10% of what happens and 90% of how we react. It is crucial to accept that we are in charge of our own attitudes and how we deal with every situation.

The following chart on attitude outlines our chances of success:

DEGREES OF POSITIVENESS RELATED TO
CHANCES FOR SUCCESS.

ATTITUDE	CHANCE OF SUCCESS (%)
I won't	0
I can't	10
I don't know how	20
I wish I could	30
I want to	40
I think I might	50
I might	60
I think I can	70
I can	80
I will	90
I did	100

Source: author unknown

Everyone Must Feel Valued

> **"**
> In the long run, the pessimist may be proven right, but the *optimist* has a better time on the trip!
> **Author unknown**
> **"**

An FSS is known for recognizing that the emotional dimension of learning and teaching is at the core of the mission statement and climate. A mission statement is short yet clear, succinct, and easy to remember. It sends the message to everyone that students and learning are *valued*. The emotional climate is essential.

Kindra Teale writes in her article "How I Make Every Student Feel Valued in My Classroom" that she is a "PROUD teacher who believes the noble profession is a craft which is honed through live experience and HEART. Every day I drive to work, I repeat the same mantra-prayer in my head. PLEASE help my mind find the right words when I feel challenged or impatient, show no malice when a middle schooler tells me to F-off – again, keep my sense of humor, be a good listener, teach my content area well and above all else, look into the eyes of each student with KINDNESS." KINDNESS is the key to everything shared. You go, girl.

Kindra has it in a nutshell. She is making her students feel valued. Do *you* have a daily mantra? An example is the one I use every day preparing for my middle school students: Too BLESSED to be STRESSED, Too EQUIPPED to be WHIPPED, and Too ANOINTED to be DISAPPOINTED.

When I meet my students on the first day of school, I have them answer the following questionnaire.

❖ Name: _____ What to call you: _____

❖ A special talent I have is:

❖ # of brothers: _____ # of sisters: _____

❖ Something about your family:

❖ Respectful means:

   Responsible means:

   Ready means:

❖ My birthday is:

❖ My favorite color is:

❖ My favorite food is:

❖ My favorite subject is:

❖ My favorite teacher is _____ because:

❖ Who is a hero in your life?

❖ What do you want to do after high school?

❖ I wish:

❖ School is:

❖ I love:

❖ The most fun I have is when I:

❖ Math is:

❖ I'm happiest when:

❖ A gift/reward that I would work hard to earn is:

❖ I'm thankful for:

❖ Actions that teachers take to F.E.E.D me:

❖ TEN other facts you need to know about me:

_____

_____

_____

_____

_____

_____

This gives me an overview of each student in my class. I have them complete it again in April to see what has changed. A climate focused on dignity and respect where everyone is valued ultimately develops the positive relationships we hunger to establish.

F.O.O.D (Fulfilling Opportunities Offered Daily) for Thought

Following are specific activities and ideas that can be implemented to reinforce how to F.E.E.D. students so they don't S.T.A.R.V.E.:

■ At each table of teams identify the definition of each term (dignity and respect), three activities already in place that emphasize dignity and respect, and one activity that each adult personally does to emphasize dignity and respect.

- Have teams identify qualities of a meaningful relationship in a staff meeting. Share and have a discussion on building relationships with students.

- Encourage random acts of kindness in students and adults. Create an "I saw you being KIND today" certificate to give out to students caught being kind. They can go to the office to share with the administration and receive a reward.

- Discuss the history of Native Americans with students. Share the Native American Code of Ethics and discuss each blessing:

Rise with the sun to pray. Pray alone. Pray often. The Great Spirit will listen, if you only speak.

Be tolerant of those who are lost on their path. Ignorance, conceit, anger, jealousy, and greed stem from a lost soul. Pray that they will find guidance.

Search for yourself, by yourself. Do not allow others to make your path for you. It is your road, and yours alone. Others may walk it with you, but no one can walk it for you.

Treat the guests in your home with much consideration. Serve them the best food, give them the best bed, and treat them with respect and honor.

Do not take what is not yours, whether from a person, a community, the wilderness, or from a culture. It was not earned nor given. It is not yours.

Respect all things that are placed upon this earth. Whether it be people or plants.

Honor other people's thoughts, wishes, and words. Never interrupt another or mock or rudely mimic them. Allow each person the right to personal expression.

Never speak of others in a bad way. The negative energy that you put out into the universe will multiply when it returns to you.

> "
> A positive attitude may not solve all of your problems, but it will annoy enough people to make it worth the effort!
> **Herm Albright**
> "

All persons make mistakes. And all mistakes can be forgiven.

Bad thoughts cause illness of the mind, body, and spirit. Practice optimism.

Nature is not FOR us, it is a PART of us. Animals, plants, and other living creatures are all part of your worldly family.

Children are the seeds of our future. Plant love in their hearts and water them with wisdom and life's lessons. When they are grown, give them space to grow.

- Conduct a "Respect Survey" for every adult and student in the FSS during the first or second month of school and as needed throughout the year. This survey requests the following:

  ✓ Do you consider yourself a respectful person?

  ✓ What do you do to demonstrate respect to others?

  ✓ What disrespectful acts have you observed personally and toward others?

TEN ACTIONS

MY BEST TEACHERS DID TO F.E.E.D. ME

1. Experience things deeply.

2. Let us express ourselves.

3. Let us know it was OK to ask questions.

4. Let us know it was OK to not understand at first.

5. Told us it was OK to be different.

6. Told us it was OK to have different opinions.

7. Let us know it was OK to stand out.

8. Always kept us in good spirits.

9. Taught us to always have a positive outlook on life.

10. Taught us there is no cure for ignorance.

To | Mrs. Reynolds, Mrs. Whittaker,
     | Mrs. Eubanks, Mrs. New
by | Joy Taylor, 9th grade

- ✓ Did you report the disrespectful acts to an adult? If no, why? If yes, was it corrected?

- ✓ What suggestions do you have to make our school more respectful?

- Develop your daily mantra like Kindra Teale did, and repeat it daily.

- Develop a questionnaire to give to your students on the *first day* so you get to know them personally. You can refer back to their answers throughout the year. Complete the same questionnaire at the end of the school year and have them compare their own answers.

- View this video at a staff meeting – https://www.teachingchannel. org/videos/teacher-student-relationship – and discuss the passion of teaching.

Now that we have the best climate and culture and a caring environment for all students, we must create an ambiance of care, comfort, and cleanliness to F.E.E.D. the students.

Jon Gordon posted, "In the spirit of MLK Day, here are 14 of my favorite **Martin Luther King Jr.** quotes." Visit http://www.jongordon.com/positivetip/ mlk.html for some wonderful inspiration!

The longer I live, the more I realize the impact of attitude on life. Attitude, to me, is more important than facts. It is more important than the past, than education, than money, than circumstances, than failure, than successes, that what other people think or say or do. It is more important than appearance, giftedness, or skill. It will make or break a company. . .a church. . . .a home. The remarkable thing is we have a CHOICE every day regarding the attitude we will EMBRACE for that day. We cannot change our past. . .we cannot change the inevitable. The only thing we can do is play on the one string we have and that is our attitude. I am convinced that life is 10% what happens to me and 90% how I react to it. And so it is with you. . . .we are in charge of our ATTITUDES.

Charles Swindoll

To laugh often and much; to win the respect of intelligent people and affection of children; to earn the appreciation of honest critics and endure the betrayal of false friends; to appreciate beauty; to find the best in others; to leave the world a better place, whether by a healthy child, a garden patch, or redeemed social condition; to know that even one life has breathed easier because you have lived. This is to have succeeded.

Ralph Waldo Emerson

You are what you do, not what you say you do.

C.G. Jung

CHAPTER 2

Ambiance: A Positive Climate and Culture

A Climate Where Everybody Is Somebody

A five-star restaurant thrives on care, comfort, good food, atmosphere, and cleanliness. When patrons are asked what they expect in a five-star restaurant they reply without hesitation: fabulous service, fabulous food and atmosphere, and a fabulously clean facility that is well kept. In some five-star restaurants, the kitchen is open and visible for all to see. This represents a restaurant with management who is entirely confident of their services and is transparent. Del Frisco's has the following statement visible: "At Del Frisco's Steakhouse we want to make your dining experience memorable." It is evident to all that care, comfort wellness, positiveness, and cleanliness are major priorities.

In five-star schools (FSSs) the custodians are valuable members of the schoolwide team and take personal pride in the facility. Custodians who feel appreciated will go above and beyond to help you keep your area fresh and orderly. Staff and students voluntarily pick up paper and trash that they see in the hallways and grounds rather than stepping over it.

It goes without saying that when we go to a five-star restaurant, we expect the entire facility to be *clean*. The same goes with five-star schools. *Cleanliness is not an option* in my opinion. When you visit schools that take satisfaction in the cleanliness of the entire school from the restrooms to the locker rooms, you can FEEL the pride of all. I once consulted at the high school and middle school in Yankton, South Dakota. Not only did the custodial staff personally greet and welcome me to both schools, you could also observe their fine work and fulfillment with the job well done. They were professional, helpful, and definitely a member of the school family. Make sure you treat the custodial staff with the care and considerations so they take pride in their jobs. They can become your best friends. They also contribute to the climate of the school.

TEN ACTIONS

MY BEST TEACHERS DID TO F.E.E.D. ME

1. She was a significant role model to me.

2. Very understanding.

3. Disciplined when necessary!

4. Actually care about my education.

5. She told me how much she loves and cares for me.

6. Encourages me to reach my highest potential.

7. She opened a world of possibility and made learning FUN!

8. She's not only my "teacher" – she was a mentor, friend, and supporter.

9. Helped me discover a passion in liking math.

10. I grew on to her and love her very much.

★MENU★

To | Mrs. Cindy Harrell
by | Taniyah Butler, 10th grade

Climate

Therefore, we must look to the "five-star philosophy" in developing the ambiance or climate of the school. It starts with believing that our students deserve a five-star experience of caring, quality, culture, and spotlessness. The FSS displays a climate of high expectations by all: that all students can learn and become productive citizens. There is a difference in *climate* and *culture*. Climate is the communication of behaviors, expectations, and interactions (NOW) and culture is the commanding source of influence to bring about effective change in schools (OVER TIME and ONGOING).

> " Do not go where the path may lead; go instead where there is no path and leave a trail.
> **Ralph Waldo Emerson** "

Five-star restaurants have indicators of "Welcome!" everywhere. Five-star schools are comparable with the emphasis on dignity and respect toward all. A great school that recognizes the importance of a welcoming atmosphere displays signs of appreciation and gratitude all over the school.

As you enter a five-star school, you immediately get the message that "We are glad you are here!" The atmosphere is pleasant. A "Welcome to our building" sign exists that *positively* invites any newcomers to stop by the front office and let them know you are here (as opposed to a sign that says something like: "Visitors who don't stop by the front office FIRST to sign in will be tackled, hog-tied, tarred, and feathered by our administrative assistant(s)"). Signs, posters, and messages throughout the hallways, offices, and classrooms indicate an environment where "Everybody is somebody." Positive etiquette is emphasized and modeled by all. My mother used to share a rhyme with me as a child to accentuate the importance of manners: "To be successful, there are two keys – the first is thank you, the other is please." I laminated this rhyme and hung it in every one of my classrooms.

The people who work in the front office are vital in creating this welcoming ambiance. Each person must have a happy tone in her/his hello and greet anyone entering with a smile and positivity. I have visited schools where soft music played in the background in the morning and during breaks to create a pleasing atmosphere, and bouquets of flowers (donated by a local florist – great advertisement) added to the experience. Do not put a person who munches and thrives on "lemon sandwiches" (people who are cranky, irritable, with limited people skills) as the initial meeter and greeter at your school.

Mrs. Gwen Scott-Morrow, the administrative assistant (AA), is the ambassador for MacIntyre Park Middle School (MPMS), where I teach, and the first person you see upon entering. She is *amazing*. She is on her second and third generation of students. She knows everyone (parents, grandparents, relatives, guardians) by name and is the happiest, most connected person I have ever met. She sets the bar high as the first person you meet in the school. Mrs. Scott-Morrow always has an authentic smile and loves the students and her job. She meets all of the criteria for the GREATEST AA I've ever worked with. She also mentors the girls in a "Smart Girls" after-school program five days a week. Mrs. Scott-Morrow is the epitome of showing "welcome" and setting the tone.

Signs of student work, walls of fame, positive posters, and someone to assist visitors are all evident at MPMS. "We are here to promote success" is the mantra, and all adults join in welcoming everyone every day. We will treat everyone with dignity and respect no matter who you are or where you come from – *diversity is divine* rings true! The adults genuinely walk it, talk it, and model it with authenticity.

The new principal at MPMS, Dr. Tret Witherspoon (following another extraordinary principal, Mrs. Tina McBride), begins every morning

> " A school's culture has far more influence on life and learning in the schoolhouse than the state department of education, the superintendent, the school board, or even the principal can ever have.
>
> **Roland Barth** "

positively and sets the tone for the day during the announcements. Sometimes he plays music that the kids love; other times he just begins. He initiates with the announcements for the day that affect students and staff. He then adds the QUOTE of the day, the WORD for the week (that teachers write on their whiteboard and refer to daily), the JOKE of the day (kids act like it's silly but they love it), sometimes a "THIS DAY IN HISTORY" segment, and reviews the BEHAVIOR expectations of the school: Be Respectful, Be Responsible, Be Ready. He concludes by naming students and adults who have birthdays and asks students to come to the front office for their special day and receive a treat. It is a positive, upbeat way to start the day.

In five-star schools where adults F.E.E.D. (Fuel, Engage, Empower Daily) the welcome spirit continues from the first day of school until the last. A truly student-oriented school has a "welcome to our school plan" that is ongoing, no matter what time of year a new student arrives. There is nothing more unnerving for a student (no matter what age or grade) to be the new kid in school. The best schools have a plan that pairs the new student with a student mentor to "hang with" for the first week to get used to the school and "in" with the right crowd.

I believe it is so unfair to a new student who is tossed a student handbook, introduced to some adults, given a schedule, and thrust into the fishbowl of a classroom with a group of strangers staring and judging. Even as adults, it is frightening when we enter a new job or experience. Think about a situation where you did not feel a comfortable fit. What was it like? What was your initial response? What were you thinking? Think of all the emotions that were being awakened. Being a new student in a new school can be horrifying if a plan is not in place to ensure success. And students are our TREASURES.

Elements of Climate

The climate of a five-star school supports the following:

✓ There is G.O.L.D. (gratitude, optimism, love, dignity) in every person. Sometimes we have to dig through a lot of dirt to get to the G.O.L.D. – but it is there.

✓ Our students did *not* select their home-life, family, race, intellect, or status in the community – they were born into it. Sometimes when I see a student being "put down" or humiliated, I want to give them a shirt that reads "Don't hate me for things I had no control over."

✓ We will work together as teams to instill in students the importance of dignity, respect, care, compassion, and tolerance. We WILL recognize this as a major priority.

✓ We can teach students from situations lacking structure the appropriate behaviors, actions, and manners. It begins with modeling as opposed to nagging. A valued friend, Dr. Dudley Flood, does a keynote address titled "Diverse Does Not Mean Deficient." Five-star schools celebrate diversity (and not just in the month of February) throughout the year.

✓ To gain respect, we must give respect. Students must see the adults in the building being kind and courteous to one another serving as role models.

✓ We will work together to solve problems and implement solutions. We won't criticize someone for who she/he is, where she/he lives, or any personal background.

✓ A climate of dignity and respect improves working conditions, increases student self-esteem/concept, and even correlates with student achievement.

✓ We will work as hard as possible to be consistent and fair to all. Mr. Jim Buysse, former outstanding principal of St. Claire High School, Minnesota, always said to his staff, "You can't treat students all the same because they are all different. But you can treat them *all fairly.*" He modeled the importance of teamwork and fairness. Again, teamwork is essential to provide consistency, which is difficult to accomplish on a regular basis.

✓ We will be free from negative discrimination and understand that we will really never understand another person until we have actually walked in their shoes. Know your customer – the students.

✓ Whenever possible – we will AVOID conflict and confrontations. Always search for the most peaceful and calm way to work through an uncomfortable situation.

You never want to get into an argument with a student; it's like mud-wrestling a pig. You *both* get dirty but the pig loves it!

✓ Teach students to be trustworthy, truthful, listeners, and their *personal best.* Teaching students how to be great listeners is so effective.

✓ Laugh every day. A day without laughter is a day not truly lived to the maximum. Have an "L" of a day EVERYDAY. I will continually address the importance of humor and laughter in the book because I believe it is one of the most important ingredients in a five-star school and in LIFE.

Just like a fine-dining experience – you want the same quality of service at the end of the meal/school year as you received at the beginning. Five-star schools maintain and sustain the feeling of *welcome, dignity,* and *respect* every single day until the last day of the school year, and the school year does not end after testing. The administration of a school with an encouraging climate:

- Provides students with a safe environment so they all can engage in the learning process and school activities.

- Celebrates staff and students daily.

- Gives teachers and support staff the tools and resources to be effective and get the job done.

- Allows all to take risks, focus on the optimistic, and provide opportunities for all.

- Engages parents and the community and provides an "invitational environment" (William Purkey).

- Sees challenges as opportunities, not obstacles.

- Has a positive culture.

Culture

Succinctly stated, the *climate* is the groups' attitude, differs from Monday to Friday, is easy to alter, establishes a state of mind, is based on perceptions, can be felt when you enter the school, is the first thing that progresses when positive change is made, and is the way everyone FEELS. By contrast, the *culture* is the group's personality, stipulates a limited way of thinking, is built on values and beliefs, can't be *felt*, is a slice of us, is the way we do things around here, and regulates whether excellence is achievable.

> " Organizational cultures are created by leaders, and one of the most decisive functions of leadership may well be the creation, the management, and – if and when that may become necessary – the destruction of culture.
> **Edgar Schein** "

In their 2010 book *Rework,* Jason Fried and David Heinemeier Hansson, co-founders of software company 37signals, wrote,

"You don't create a culture. Culture happens. It's the by-product of consistent behavior. If you encourage people to share, and you give them the freedom to share, then sharing will be built into your culture. If you reward trust then trust will be built into your culture."

Thomas J. Sergiovanni said, "Culture is the most powerful source of leverage for bringing about change in a school – or any organization, for that matter." In 1999, Terrence Deal and Kent Peterson wrote *Shaping School Culture: The Heart of Leadership*. They define school culture this way:

> " Culture is the underground stream of norms, values, beliefs, traditions, and rituals that builds up over time as people work together, solve problems, and confront challenges. This set of informal expectations and values shapes how people think, feel, and act in schools.
> **Deal and Peterson** "

> *Culture* provides a more accurate and intuitively appealing way to help student leaders to understand their own school's unwritten rules and traditions, norms and expectations that seem to permeate everything; the way people act, dress, what they talk about or avoid talking about, whether they seek out colleagues for help or don't, and how teachers feel about their work and their students.

It's not easy to tell the staff of a school to change your culture – it is rooted deeply in people. "It is embodied in their attitudes, values, and skills, which in turn stem from their personal background, life experiences, and from the community they belong to" (Margaret B. Arbuckle, former executive director of the Guilford Education Alliance). It generally refers to beliefs, perceptions, relationships, and attitudes that shape and influence how a school operates. Student performance will never improve until the school culture is one "where people feel valued, safe, and share the goal of self-improvement," according to Dr. Christopher Wagner, co-director of the Center for Improving School Culture.

The following list shared by Judith Sanders Enright represents traits commonly connected to positive school culture:

- The individual successes of teachers and students are recognized and celebrated.

- Staff relationships are collegial, collaborative, and productive, and all staff members are held to high professional standards.

- Students and staff members feel emotionally and physical safe, and the school's policies and facilities promote student safety.

- School leaders, teachers, and staff members model positive, healthy behaviors for students.

- Mistakes are not considered as failures, but they are seen as opportunities to learn and grow for both students and educators.

- Students are consistently held to high academic expectations, and a majority of students meet or exceed those expectations.

- Important leadership decisions are made collaboratively with input from staff members, students, and parents.

- Criticism, when voiced, is constructive and well intentioned, not antagonistic, or self-serving.

- Educational resources and learning opportunities are equally distributed, and all students, including minorities and students with disabilities, have access to these resources.

- All students have access to the academic support and services they may need to succeed.

The following describe a few representative examples of common ways that schools may attempt to improve their culture:

- Establish *professional learning communities* (PLCs) that encourage teachers to communicate, share expertise, and work together more collegially and productively.

- Provide presentations, seminars, professional development, and learning experiences designed to educate staff and students about bullying and ways to reduce instances of bullying.

- Create events and educational experiences that honor and celebrate the racial, ethnic, and linguistic diversity of the student body.

- Establish an *advocacy/advisory program* that pairs groups of students with adult advisors to strengthen adult-student relationships and ensure that students are well known and supported by at least one adult in the school. The program continues throughout the entire school year.

- Survey students, parents, and teachers about their experiences in the school, and host community forums that invite participants to share their opinions about and recommendations for the school and its programs.

- Create a *leadership team* comprising a representative cross-section of school administrators, teachers, students, parents, and community members that oversees and leads a school-improvement committee.

Dr. Thomas Lickona (*Educating for Character*) states, "Throughout history, education has had two main goals; to help people become smarter and to help people become good." A positive *climate* and *culture* addresses both.

F.O.O.D (Fulfilling Opportunities Offered Daily) for Thought

The following ideas and activities are listed as possible ways to F.E.E.D. all students so they don't S.T.A.R.V.E. (Stop Trying And Reject Valuable Education) and develop a five-star school:

> ➤ Have a "wall of fame" of pictures of all the adults in the building when they were in elementary, middle, and/or high school. Devise a contest for the students to guess the adult in the picture.

> ➤ Have a "caught you caring" wall in the front entrance and post pictures each month of students doing kind things for others (ask a local establishment to donate the cameras and develop the pictures).

> ➤ Decorate the front office with "happy symbols" like flowers (donated by local florists), music, positive sayings, and happiness.

> ➤ Have all adults project happiness in their hello and openly greet one another and students each day (you don't have to love your colleagues and have "staff sleep-overs" – just be pleasant).

> ➤ Have a "Celebrate Custodians, Food Service Workers, Para Professionals, and other non-certificated staff members day" throughout the year where everyone thanks the individuals for making the school a happy and inviting facility.

> ➤ Have a "15-second rule" (or what works for your staff) in the front office: no human being will EVER stand in the front office for longer than [X] seconds before someone *happily* asks, "Can I assist you?"

> ➤ At a staff meeting, take time for teams to discuss what a positive climate means to the faculty. Identify the schoolwide and team activities ongoing that month that focus on a positive climate.

> **"**
> The school culture dictates in no uncertain terms "the way we do things around here." Ultimately, a school's culture has far more influence on life and learning in the school than the state department of education, the superintendent, the school board, or even the principal can ever have.
>
> **Roland Barth**
> **"**

> **"**
> A school's culture is its more enduring aspect. The explicit rules of the school the policies and procedures, feel much more "tangible," but they are also much easier to change. An administrator can change the rules with a decree. But you can't tell the staff of a school to "Change your culture!" Culture is rooted deeply in people. It is embodied in their attitudes, values, and skills, which in turn stem from their personal background, life experiences and from the communities they belong to.
>
> **Margaret Arbuckle**
> **"**

➤ As a staff, identify your own guidelines for creating a positive atmosphere. Teach these guidelines to the students and consistently monitor the strategies. Cover the classroom walls with signs to remind students to be kind to one another.

➤ Establish a "Dine with Dignity" program that emphasizes students eating with new students, watching out for students with special needs, and taking care of the dining area while practicing respectable manners.

➤ Ask every student and adult in the student to write their favorite positive statement (either personal or by someone else – giving credit of course) on a poster board that they decorate and the staff laminates to hang throughout the school. Include the student's name, author's name if not the student, and any fun fact that the student wants to share. Add more when new students arrive and ask the students and adults for new posters ever three or four months (or whatever is reasonable). Bombard your hallways and classrooms with positive messages.

➤ Develop a positive plan with a "meeters and greeters" program for interested students. The meeters and greeters are available to escort visitors that enter the school around the building and show them the highlights of the facility. They also introduce the visitors to staff members and answer questions (also have a *safety plan* to acknowledge when there are visitors in the school).

➤ Begin every school year with a theme for the year. Have the students help decide the theme. A yearlong theme builds spirit, motivates students and staff, and provides focus. Some sample themes can include:

- *Respect.* Play the song on a continual basis.

- *Reach for the stars.* Encouraging everyone to be a STAR.

- *Celebrate.* Where success is continuously celebrated and of course the day can start with Kool & the Gang's song "Celebration."

- Take one step at a time.

- Sail into learning with a nautical theme.

- Destination learning.

- Dream, Dare, Do, and Don't Forget to Dance.

➤ Have an annual schoolwide motto and logo that support the annual theme. Include a song and have monthly activities that emphasize the slogan. An example of a motto would be my favorite Napoleon Hill's quote, "If you can conceive it and believe it you can achieve it." The theme song could be "Ain't No Mountain High Enough," and the logo could be a mountain. Draw on students to develop this each year.

➤ Develop sayings and a poster at the entrance that could say:

"Can our school be so welcoming, so inviting, and so comfortable that every person who walks through our doors believes they are about to have an amazing experience?"

(Author unknown)

➤ Develop a "New Team Member" plan to make new staff feel welcomed and appreciated.

➤ Develop a teacher's pledge by your staff that commits to creating a positive climate. An example is from Rivera High School, Brownsville, Texas:

1. I will welcome each student every day.

2. I believe in you.

3. I will listen and be available.

4. I will recognize and praise my students and challenge each student to reach their potential.

5. I will be fair, consistent, and respectful.

6. I will model good character by being professional, enthusiastic, and admitting when I am wrong.

7. I will create a positive learning environment by being patient, supportive, and understanding.

8. I will be passionate and knowledgeable about my subject and provide quality assignments daily.

9. I will give constructive feedback in a timely manner.

10. I will provide creative opportunities for learning.

➤ Assess your climate. Five-star schools assess the climate, culture, and environment of the school. A simple evaluation can be to ask teachers the following questions:

1. Do all students get recognized positively at some point during the year?

2. Is there a plan in place to ensure that all students receive some form of encouraging appreciation throughout the year?

3. Do students see teachers interacting positively and politely with one another?

4. Do you truly believe that all students can learn and failure is not fatal?

5. Is our school appealing to all, ensuring an atmosphere of welcome and inspiration?

6. Do all students have at least one adult they can approach in time of need or assistance?

7. Is a common core of respect and constructive relationship building evident?

8. Do you talk *calmly* to students? Yelling and screaming do not fix the problem. (A student once told me that when his teachers shout at him, he switches the channel.)

9. Is there a supportive schoolwide team in place where everyone respects others' position, responsibilities, background, culture, and attitude?

After having the teachers complete the above individually, an opportunity to break into groups and debate answers is imperative. After rich discussions, small groups then can begin to develop the common core of beliefs concerning the climate of the school.

Develop a yearlong "new student" plan using other students as mentors and helping new students feel welcomed and appreciated.

Review the "Ten Commandments of How to Have an 'L' of a Day Through Living, Learning, Loving, and Laughing" and have teams develop their own list:

1. *Remain open-minded and flexible.* Discuss but do not argue. Sometimes we have to agree to disagree and move on.

2. *Do not say anything to anyone that you would not want said to you.* We all have feelings and we need to be considerate to those feelings.

3. *"Seek first to understand and then to be understood"* (Covey). Try to put yourself in other peoples' place to recognize where they are coming from.

4. *Remember to laugh.* No one has ever died from laughing. Maintain a sense of humor and wit. Instead of saying, "I will laugh about this someday," laugh about it today.

5. *Eleanor Roosevelt said, "No one can make you feel inferior without your consent."* Do not let negative people bring you down to their level – rise above it. Spend your day around encouraging people.

6. *Make a point to focus on the positive in all situations.* Be a person filled with life and vitality. Reflect at the end of each day on the positive interactions and conversations you had with an attitude of gratitude.

7. *Live by the adage, "If you don't have something good to say about a person or situation, do not say anything at all."* My mother truly lived by that wise saying. Avoid gossip and putting others down. Use "put-ups."

8. *Look for the best in people.* Ask about their interests and pursuits.

9. *Be an all-out WINNER.* Dress, act, walk, speak, and live like a champion with an attitude of gratitude.

10. *Live each day to the fullest with a* T.G.I.T. *(thank goodness it's today) outlook.* Do not dwell on failures – focus on accomplishments and successes (success is failure turned inside out).

Recognize each day differently and challenge teachers and students to celebrate the daily theme: for example, Magnificent Monday, Terrific Tuesday, Wonderful Wednesday, Thankful Thursday, and Fabulous Friday. Have the staff and students develop other daily themes. At MPMS, Dr. Witherspoon encourages students and adults to have fun by dressing to the daily themes. An example is:

Celebrity Monday. Come dressed as your favorite celebrity.

Tie Tuesday. All boys are encouraged to wear ties or bowties and dress for success.

Wacky Wednesday. Everyone dresses up looking "wacky."

ESPN Thursday. Come dressed as someone you see on ESPN (the TV sports channel).

Fan Friday. Come dressed celebrating your favorite college or professional sports team.

Now that we have developed a positive, student-centered climate and culture, let's forge ahead to ensure students are provided a safe environment through specific ingredients.

> **"**
> For yesterday is but a dream and tomorrow is only a vision but today well lived makes every yesterday a dream of happiness and every tomorrow a vision of hope. Look well, therefore to this day.
> **Sir William Osler**
> **"**

Can our school be so welcoming, so inviting, and so comfortable that everyone who walks through the door believes he/she is about to have an amazing experience?

Climate:

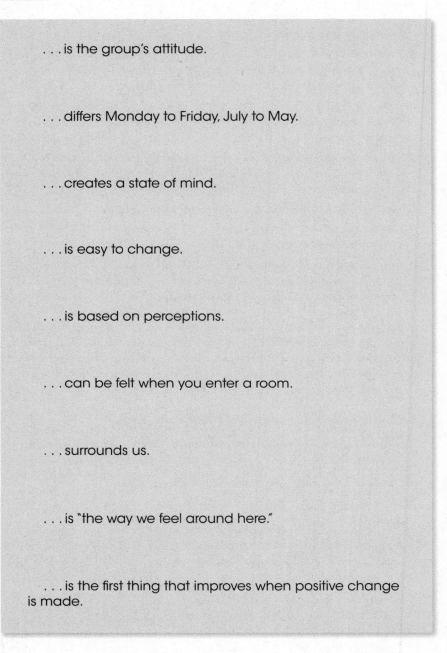

. . . is the group's attitude.

. . . differs Monday to Friday, July to May.

. . . creates a state of mind.

. . . is easy to change.

. . . is based on perceptions.

. . . can be felt when you enter a room.

. . . surrounds us.

. . . is "the way we feel around here."

. . . is the first thing that improves when positive change is made.

CHAPTER 3

Safety: Physical, Emotional, Social, and Intellectual

A Safe Environment for Students Exists

The last time that you went to a five-star restaurant, did you even *think* about safety or discuss it on the ride to the establishment? Of course not. We just know it will be fine because it has a fabulous reputation and nothing has ever happened before. You assume the food is safe, that the servers are spick-and-span and have washed their hands, and there are fire extinguishers in the kitchen – JUST IN CASE. Your experience, in most cases, is peaceful and safe with little disturbances or hazardous circumstances.

Five-star schools must always concentrate on safety and have a plan in place to deal with any unsafe circumstances. On the contrary, we hear of horrific acts of violence on a regular basis. Unfortunately, many educators hear of school shootings and other unspeakable acts of violence and think: "That would *never* happen here." We can't think like that anymore. Violence can happen anywhere. Every school must have a plan in place.

Our number-one priority in schools is to ensure that students, parents, and community members will all be secure in *our* school. We are serving students from all types of homes; from dysfunctional to "no parent at home" to first-class living. We serve a total range from poverty to special needs to entitled and gifted. We see pregnant teenagers, racism, drug trafficking, weapons, suicide, dealing with sexual identity, and the most rampant – BULLYING. We have to be so aware of our surroundings, our students, our visitors, and the ambiance of the school.

So many problems not only endanger students and teachers but also prevent teachers from concentrating on teaching and students from concentrating on learning. We need tools, strategies, leadership, and community support that enhance the safety and success of all students and adults. We want a protected, secure, peaceful, learning setting.

A Safe and Secure Environment

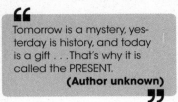

"
Tomorrow is a mystery, yesterday is history, and today is a gift . . .That's why it is called the PRESENT.
(Author unknown)
"

Where do you feel safe? What mechanisms are necessary to make you feel safe? Have you ever felt as though your safety was being compromised? Especially in this time of bullying, sexting, cyberbullying, and social media explosion, our students sometimes have a difficult time focusing. Any child who doesn't feel safe will have trouble learning. The school climate is a critical aspect to learning. All research finds a positive correlation between positive school climate and increased student achievement. And safety is not only physical – it is social, emotional, and intellectual as well.

Teachers can do so much to create a climate of well-being for all. They must be aware of the emotions that are the foundation for inappropriate behavior and deal with this conduct immediately. They must concentrate on consistency and integrity, teach the appropriate behavior starting the first day of the school year, and assure students that they are safe. Learning to identify the causes that set off the fight-flight-fright emotions, teacher and students together can learn how to differ any negative responses.

Tamara Fyke states, "Terror attacks, mass shootings, and natural catastrophes fill the news on almost a daily basis. We may or may not be directly impacted but the reality shows that we need safe climates and caring adults in schools more than ever."

Throughout this chapter we will allude to the importance of adults taking a hard look at the core of safety, which includes *bullying, motivation,* and *discipline.* Each topic is a *piece of the pie that connects directly to security.*

Summarizing many research studies, the general qualities of safe schools include:

➤ High expectations and standards of rigor, relevance, relationships, and richness:

- *Teaching is a serious business.* All teachers must let students know from the first day of school that they have high expectations and expect the best. A curriculum of rigor will be enforced.

- *Teachers must accentuate relevance.* When students don't see the connections or the use of information in their life, they shut down. Curriculum must be reality-based and provide life-long skills for students to practice. For example, one of the most important skills student need to learn is dealing with finance, writing a check, budgeting their money, and all of the components of being a shrewd saver.

- *Relationships are the foundation of a safe climate, environment, and culture.* Teachers must be willing to develop professional and mentoring relationships with students. They don't need to be friends of the students – students should find their friends in their peers.

- Teachers must provide rich experiences that involve students, provide connections, and support them in preparing for a profitable future as an adult.

➤ Schoolwide "steps for success" that are based on integrity and respect:

- A five-star school has a schoolwide discipline policy that focuses on what you must do correctly, not what you are caught doing wrong. *Top-chef teachers* let students know that misbehavior won't be accepted and realistic consequences will be applied. Students are *taught* and *shown* what good behavior looks like.

- All consequences must be given with honesty and value. A five-star school believes that to obtain respect from students, they first must receive it.

➤ A detailed plan for crisis and emergency situations:

- Every school in today's world *must* have a crisis and emergency plan in place. Everyone needs to be informed and aware. Too often after a crisis, someone is seen saying, "We never thought it could happen here." There must be a code word used over the intercom to relay to adults that they need a lock down and there may be a problem, or even just say "lock down," which gives a strong message.

- Teachers are preventative and are trained to recognize crisis situations. They never hesitate reporting a concern or possible violation (there are many models of crisis plans available on the web). **Never take a threat lightly.**

➤ Adults who are visible and available for students to share concerns:

- Five-star schools insist that teachers are always visible in hallways, cafeterias, gymnasiums, restrooms, school grounds, and throughout the building. If you are fortunate enough to have resource officers, they must be obvious throughout the school, in restrooms, and especially walking the hallways during class changes.

- A five-star school ensures that every student has at least one adult he or she can turn to in case of an emergency, an uncomfortable situation, or fear.

➤ A strategy that addresses any form of bullying and the consequences:

- Five-star schools make it known that no form of bullying is acceptable; there is *zero tolerance.*

- Teachers ensure that students feel comfortable reporting acts of bullying or any form of harassment.

- A schoolwide policy is in place with predetermined penalties for major infractions. The guidelines are austere and are enforceable with no areas of confusions or question.

- Consistency and strictness are strong drivers of the mission and goals of the school.

- Teachers don't ignore any signs of bullying occurring in the school and make a commitment to be unfailing in averting bullying.

- Teachers work with students to resolve conflicts and settle disagreements. When a conflict arises, they learn to first acknowledge it, stop, breathe, and think about the action to take.

- Again, the message of the school is, "Being CRUEL is not COOL."

➤ High levels of parent involvement:

- Five-star schools do whatever it takes to involve as many parents as possible via email, newsletters, meetings, and websites.

- Teachers make it a priority to begin each year by linking positively with a group of parents to begin a connection.

- Parents are continuously invited for input, suggestions, and ways to put into practice a five-star school.

- Parents or guardians are called immediately when there is a concern about their child.

- The first weeks of school, teachers contact parents with a positive statement about their children. If you begin with a positive connection, the parents will be more likely to work with you during the year.

- Parent meetings are held regularly. Components of effective meetings to get parents to attend include a time that is convenient for parents, food, a small concert or performance by students, child care for smaller children (with high school students monitoring the room), and door prizes. If your school is fortunate enough to have an on-staff person in charge of parent connections, she/he needs to be relentless in discovering what gets parents to the meetings.

➤ Ongoing partnerships with the community:

- Five-star schools invest heavily in the community by making connections and inviting community members to be on advisory committees, talk to students, and participate in school activities.

- Teachers ask community leaders to be mentors to students, share experiences, and contribute services and donations for student and teacher incentives.

- Community members are invited to special events and are given a few minutes to state their business and appreciation for education.

> I have come to a frightening conclusion that I am the decisive element in the classroom. It's my personal approach that creates the climate. It is my daily mood that makes the weather. As a teacher, I possess the tremendous power to make a student's life miserable or joyous. I can be a tool of torture, or an instrument of inspiration. I can humiliate or humor, hurt or heal. In all situations, it is my response that decides whether a crisis will be escalated or de-escalated, and a child humanized or de-humanized.
>
> **Haim Ginott**

Great schools are places where everyone first and foremost feels safe. A place that is open yet organized – where bullying and name-calling and physical violence are nonexistent. When parents are asked what they predominantly require from the school, the most frequent response is, "We want our children to be *safe*." Schools *must* create this physical environment of security for all.

Five-Star Schools Have Goals

Goals provide direction. A common set of goals provides a framework for everyone to adhere to and acknowledge. Goals provide a roadmap for student success. In five-star schools, everyone knows the goals, the importance of teaching them to students, and give attention to consistently examining the goals to F.E.E.D. (Fuel, Engage, Empower Daily) students.

Five-star schools take time to obtain input from all teachers to form annual student-focused outcome goals. In my opinion, the goals of a five-star school include but are not limited to teaching students to:

➤ Appreciate education and develop a joy of learning.

➤ *Respect who they are.* Physically, emotionally, socially, and intellectually, along with others.

➤ Realize they are responsible for their own behavior.

➢ *Learn how to learn.* The process is as important as the product.

➢ Understand the importance of trying and succeeding with failure in between.

➢ Learn how to cooperate, care, respect, and appreciate all backgrounds, cultures, diversities, and special needs.

➢ Strive to set and accomplish goals and teach students that dreams are goals with deadlines.

➢ Recognize that positive relationships set a foundation for a successful life.

➢ Realize that people, not programs are what really matter.

➢ Live each day positively to the fullest providing care and compassion to others.

Once the teachers, parents, students, and administrators in the building set the goals and focus on them daily, extraordinary things can happen. The goals of a five-star school are to create an environment that is:

✓ Positive to all

✓ Student-focused and recognizing all needs

✓ Encouraging

✓ Focused on positive behavior and respect

✓ Safe and bully-free

✓ Open to all backgrounds and diversities of life

✓ Engaging, welcoming, and encouraging

> **"** We need to seize every opportunity to give encouragement. Encouragement is oxygen to the soul.
> **Author Unknown "**

Physical Safety

Most students are reluctant to go to an adult and tell them of a bullying incident for fear of retribution. During a recent school visit, where I shadowed a fabulous principal, Cathy Egley at Richard Milburn Academy in Deland, Florida, I saw ongoing evidence of students reporting bullying that had occurred through texting and other forms of social media. Why did they feel protected going to the principal? Because Mrs. Egley and her teachers had created an environment where students feel comfortable and secure. That is what five-star school principals, administrative teams, and teachers do. Care means trust is established and you don't fear abuse or continuous harassment.

The best resources for determining the effectiveness of school policies and procedures are the students. Anytime we can get student input we learn and grow. Teachers from five-star schools conduct ongoing assessments concerning safety. Simply by asking students questions about their personal safety and feelings in general will provide valuable data. The goal must be to keep any student from "falling through the cracks" and being a part of the "schoolhouse to jailhouse" track.

We know that when we have a safe and respectful school climate there is improved student attendance, fewer behavioral problems, improved interpersonal relationships, improved academic achievement, and an overall tolerance of others. Five-star schools work toward this goal every day never forgetting Abraham Maslow's hierarchy of needs, safety/security, belonging, achievement, and self-actualization. Trust is also vital.

Trust

Trust is a major factor in a five-star school. I copied a statement (author unknown) stating, "Human beings can fix anything with enough time and enough duct tape except trust." Interpersonal trust is fundamental to the development of common beliefs and values. Without trust we become paralyzed and powerless. Creating a trustful atmosphere will move a staff to an interdependent atmosphere and F.E.E.D. the students.

Stephen Covey's 13 behaviors to establish trust include:

1. Talk straight.
2. Demonstrate respect.
3. Create transparency.
4. Right wrongs.
5. Show loyalty.
6. Deliver results.
7. Get better.
8. Confront reality.
9. Clarify expectations.
10. Practice accountability.
11. Listen first.
12. Keep commitment.
13. Extend trust.

> **"** The secret to my success? There will be five to six guys who love you. There will be five to six guys who want you fired. The rest of the guys are not sure. The goal – keep the five to six guys who hate you away from the guys who are not sure.
> **Yogi Berra "**

Deep involvement gives us opportunities to be heard, to make choices, to have obligations, to belong, and to engage in problem solving. Providing guided opportunities for participation in defining and developing trust is an important principle of compassionate teaching. Such chances can provide support, affirm self-worth, and create mutual trust.

Don't withhold trust because it involves risk. Create a trusting and nonviolent environment for all incudes major components that are the ingredients for continued success. The components address *bullying, motivation,* and *discipline.*

Bullying

Parents want their children to be safe, free from any harm of abuse, bullying, or, as we say in the south, "cracking." We can consider all the recent outcomes in the past years due to bullying. *People* magazine (October 18, 2010) dedicated 15 pages to the topic. The first article is titled "Tormented to Death?" We can't let that happen. It concludes with an article of why students are bullied due to jealousy, sexual orientation, religion, weight, or race, and because of any personal characteristic that someone can abuse.

Bullying has become an epidemic. In five-star schools, teachers say NO to bullying to F.E.E.D. students so they don't S.T.A.R.V.E. (Stop Trying And Reject Valuable Education). They provide ongoing professional development to adults discussing the following:

- ✓ *What is bullying?* Bullying is the aggressive behavior that entails unsolicited, negative actions. It entails a pattern of negative behavior recurring over time and involves a disproportion of power or intensity.

- ✓ *What can bullying look like?* With the social media on the rise, bullying comes in many forms. It can be aggressive physical behavior of kicking, hitting, name-calling, choking, and harming another. It includes derogatory comments, social exclusion or isolation, spreading lies and false rumors, have items stolen or damaged, threats or forced to do things, and the most frequent, cyberbullying with cell phones and the internet. Additionally, cyber-harassment and cyberstalking are growing and very serious crimes.

✓ *What are the statistics?* A recent article on bullying (http://www.how-to-stop-bullying.com) presented the following:

➤ School bullying statistics and cyberbullying statistics show that 77% of students are bullied mentally, verbally, and physically.

➤ 15% of high school students reported 1–3 bullying incidents in the last month, and 3.4% reported 10 times or more.

➤ 23% of elementary students reported being bullied 1–3 times in the last month.

➤ 30% of US students in grades 6–10 are involved in moderate or frequent bullying as bullies, as victims, or as both.

➤ Recent bullying statistics admit that half of all bullying incidents go unreported. Cyberbullying statistics indicate even less of these are reported.

➤ 100 000 students carry a gun to school.

➤ Each day, 160 000 student miss school for fear of being bullied.

➤ 43% fear harassment in the bathroom at school.

➤ 282 000 students are physically attacked in secondary schools each month.

➤ 54% said witnessing physical abuse at home could lead to violence in school.

➤ In a recent study, 77% of the students had been bullied. Cyber-bullying statistics expose similar numbers. And 14% of those who were bullied experienced severe reactions to the cruelty.

➤ Playground school bully statistics – every *seven* minutes a student is bullied: Adult intervention – 4%. Peer intervention – 11%. No intervention – 85%.

✓ *What can we do?* Teachers and all adults in the school must first recognize that bullying does exist. They must have current discussions about the widespread and realize it is a part of their job to watch out for any negative activities. Other suggestions include:

➤ Begin a schoolwide approach to establishing a kinder, more compassionate school. Following the devastating Columbine incident, Rachel's Challenge has helped millions of students become advocates of anti-bullying efforts.

➤ Implement an advocacy, advisory, or student-focused program where every student in the school has one adult advocate that they can go to if they are frightened, being bullied, or have concerns about other students. Depending on the needs of the teachers and students, it can be formalized or nonstructured. The key is to have a program in place that ensures students' well-being.

➤ Concentrate on student–teacher relationships where teachers try to learn as much about their students as possible. We realize in a test-absorbed world that this becomes challenging, but teachers from five-star schools are already doing it.

➤ Be visible when students are entering or exiting your classroom to pick up on any evidence of tension or stress between students. Keep your eyes and ears open and always report any concern to the principal and/or administrative team.

➤ Joe Coles, an expert on how to stop bullying, recommends we talk to the students and ask them the following questions:

  • What does bullying look like?

  • What does bullying behavior sound like?

  • How can you help a victim?

  • How can you help the bully?

  • How does bullying affect school climate and your day?

  • How do we use compassion to put an end to bullying?

  • What can each one of you do individually to end bullying?

➤ Begin an "adopt a student program" where willing teachers are assigned to noticeably distraught and disconnected students.

➤ Look at motivation issues and how to influence the unmotivated.

Motivation

Motivation is defined as the extent to which persistent effort is directed toward a goal. It comes from the Latin word *movere*, meaning to move. Motivation is the choice of an action, the determination, and the energy spent. It is responsible for why we decide to complete something, how long we are planning to maintain the interest, and how hard we will engage in obtaining the outcome. It is the initiative that encourages action or feelings, igniting the spark for engagement.

Unmotivated students can be apathetic, aggressive, disorganized, passive, rebellious, withdrawn, perfectionists, hyperactive, gifted, and/or moving. I have had a student for the last two years that truly can't stay seated. Within three to five minutes upon entering class, she is up and walking about. I realized I could not fight this, so we made a plan that she had to stay in the back of the room, not disturb any other students, and had to be on task. This worked – on some days.

Motivation starts from within. To motivate others you first must understand motivation and know how you motivate yourself. Motivation is also connected to your goals and students' goals. We truly are defined by the choices we make. We want to motivate students to make the best choices possible. Motivation must transpire from the inside out! Students are motivated when they are in a positive relationship with an adult that they admire and care about and don't want to disappoint.

> **"** Try to imagine a highly motivated scientist who has not been rewarded for doing science, a singer who has not been rewarded for singing, an inventor who has not been rewarded for inventing, a teacher who does not get paid for teaching. Outstanding achievement always produces extrinsic rewards of some kind; how else, then, do outstanding achievers maintain their motivation?
>
> **(Slavin, 1991)** **"**

Motivation is important to F.E.E.D. students so they don't S.T.A.R.V.E. Motivation is responsible for why we decide to do something, how long we will endure the activity, and how intensely are we going to practice this activity. Eric Jensen shares, "There is no such thing as an unmotivated student. There is, however, students in unmotivated circumstances." It amazes me to see a student who does practically nothing in class but put them in front of a computer, musical instrument, cheerleading squad, art class, or on a basketball court and you observe a totally different person. They *are* motivated but just not what we have in front of them.

We must inspire students' beliefs in their ability and provide a motivating sense of self. We want our students to gain confidence and see a world of hope. A top-chef teacher knows and believes that without a positive motivating environment where students feel valued and appreciated, academics become difficult to stress. We teach a failure-is-not-fatal model encouraging students to do their best, be their best, and celebrate their best. Napoleon Hill states, "Most great people have attained their greatest success just one step beyond their greatest failure." Failure can do more than build flexibility, it can help students acquire a sense of trust. We all know of intrinsic motivation and extrinsic motivation.

When I first began my career as a special education teacher, I remember believing that all of my students would be intrinsically motivated and there would be no fluff or extrinsic motivators in my classroom. It took me one week and we were striving for a *pizza party*. Extrinsic works as long as it is not expected and only given when truly deserved. Every now and then I will hand out a piece of candy to a student I see doing something kind. However, they know if they ask for it, they won't receive it.

The unmotivated student is motivated to avoid schoolwork and sometimes make a commotion during class. More work is put into avoiding academic challenges than facing them. At times, test scores can suggest high potential

> Even if the student's life away from school is bleak and miserable, he or she will work if what he or she finds in school is satisfying.
> **William Glasser**

that is not observed in daily classroom implementation. When working with unmotivated students, we must first determine who the student is – the background, family life, friends, and talents. We must determine what does motivate this student and start from there giving students ownership to the learning process. To interrupt the cycle of failure is our main goal so the student finally FEELS success and confidence. If you have never tasted chocolate, you don't know what you are missing – the same with success.

Assigning students' duties in the classroom builds community and inspires motivation. Students will see the classroom jobs as a privilege rather than a nuisance and will work hard to ensure that they, and other students, are meeting expectations. Also allow students to lead activities, solve problems on the white/smart board, act as the teacher and help out so they feel cherished and essential. My students are always asking what they can do for me.

Use "Post-it Note therapy." I am addicted to Post-it Notes. Ed Frye invented them in 1980 due to a mistake in his experiment. They have changed my life, and they can change others. I always have them with me, and when I see someone doing something positive or someone is nice to me, I write them a thank you note on a Post-it. One of my students at the end of this year showed me her notebook. She had saved EVERY Post-it Note I had given her from the first day. They are simple, cheap, and effective ways to motivate. My challenge to everyone who reads this book is to hand out three positive Post-it Notes daily (to students, colleagues, parents, support staff, and administrators) for every day that you are in school. You won't believe the return with Post-it Note therapy. Have fun!

The BEST motivators:

1. Believe students are competent and trustworthy.

2. Avoid labeling.

3. Avoid sarcasm.

4. Have high expectations.

5. LISTEN to students.

6. Avoid overemphasis on competition.

7. Focus on successes not past failures (the past doesn't equal the future).

8. Set clear goals for accomplishments and teach students how to set goals.

9. Know the five basic needs of human beings according to W. Glasser:

- – physiological needs
- – the need to belong
- – the need for freedom
- – the need for power
- – the need for FUN

Every student needs at least one adult in the building that the student feels comfortable approaching when sad, scared, worried, bullied, or when the student just needs to talk. Connections are vital. Students must feel a sense of belonging, appreciation, and admiration to the people who are important to them. When students feel a *connection* to their teachers and feel they are empathetic, encouraging, and *fun* (Chapter 10), motivation is higher, and trust has been built.

Additional tools to increase intrinsic motivation:

- ➤ Provide meaningful choices.
- ➤ Provide frequent, specific, nonjudgmental feedback dedicated to progress and growth.
- ➤ Embed learning in activities that students find enjoyable and worthwhile.
- ➤ Protect all students from embarrassment and humiliation (even from other adults if necessary).
- ➤ Build positive self-confidence through confirmation of success.
- ➤ Avoid the overuse of extrinsic motivators. Make them special and given when not expected.
- ➤ Model learning with enthusiasm.
- ➤ Work with teams to build community and a sense of ownership of the school.
- ➤ Provide celebrations for achievements.

An outstanding article ("5 Questions to Ask Yourself about Your Unmotivated Students") by Jennifer Gonzalez found that:

1. "Students are more motivated academically when they have a positive relationship with their teacher.

2. *Choice* is a powerful motivator in most educational contexts.

3. For complex tasks that require creativity and persistence, extrinsic rewards and consequences actually hamper motivation.

4. To stay motivated, to persist at any task, students must believe that can improve in that task.

5. Students are motivated to learn things that have relevance to their lives."

She further listed the five questions to ask yourself about your unmotivated students:

1. *How is your relationship with your students, REALLY?* The quality of student–teacher relationships is unequivocally the most important source for motivating the unmotivated.

2. *How much CHOICE do your students actually have?* Choice is a major influence in motivation. We know this but many have not fully incorporated it into their lessons.

3. *Are you relying heavily on carrots (rewards) and sticks (punishments) – or jolly ranchers?* We don't want students to *expect* a reward every time they do something. Be adaptable.

4. *Do your words contribute to a growth mindset or a fixed mindset?* The growth mindset is a belief that their intelligence and abilities can be developed with effort. There is so much research on the importance of the growth mindset and how it affects learning and achievement. A fixed mindset is not motivating.

5. *What are you doing to make your content relevant to student lives?* This is imperative. If you can't determine the relevancy – ask your students. It's amazing what they can come up with when challenged.

All so important. Thank you, Jennifer Gonzalez, for an extraordinary and significant article. Impressive job!

Discipline

Safety can't be addressed without discussing discipline and behavior. Again, there is a plethora of research and hundreds of books on the topics alone. However, to F.E.E.D. students appropriately, we must touch on the importance of positive, consistent, fair, and ongoing discipline in a five-star school that is protected. We want to emphasize the importance of self-discipline, self-image, self-esteem, self-concept, self-respect, and self-actualization on a daily basis. Positive behavior is doing what's best for kids and creating a safe and appropriate learning environment for all students and staff.

Dr. Sharon Faber stated, "When teachers want help with discipline today, they are looking for something far broader than a set of rules or a code of conduct to enforce in the classroom. What they truly need is a set of tools to create and maintain a calm and orderly, yet dynamic and lively climate where teaching and learning can occur." Dr. Faber said, "This climate is based on a deep understanding of the characteristics and needs of students, how students learn, a relationship of caring, respect, and trust, effective instructional strategies, and a solid repertoire of management techniques that really work." You need a cookbook filled with a set of skills that will help you build a positive environment. As Marzano states after 30 years of research:

> Classroom management is one of the critical INGREDIENTS of effective teaching. Good classroom managers are teachers who understand and use specific techniques. Awareness of, and training in these techniques, can change teacher behavior which in turn changes student behavior and ultimately affect student achievement positively . . . research evidence supports this assertion.

Schools must have a systematic atmosphere where teaching and learning are the core of the mission and vision.

In a five-star school, teachers practice positive discipline to help students develop self-discipline and a sense of boundaries, experience the consequences of negative behavior, and learn from mistakes. The purpose of positive disciplines is to teach students suitable behavior and not negatively impact self-worth. It is to protect the dignity of the person while encouraging the restructuring of adverse actions. Teachers must manage conflict civilly and teach students to take responsibility for their actions. Amie Dean, the Behavior Queen (definitely visit her website), provides faculties with many simple methods and techniques to develop a positive behavior plan. She shares the stages of the classroom discipline cycle as:

- *Reminder 1.* Nonverbal warning (the look, Post-it Note).

- *Reminder 2.* Verbal warning (positive, if you choose to continue you choose to_____).

- *Reminder 3.* Consequence menu (loss of privilege, silent lunch).

- *Reminder 4.* Consequence (parent contact, office referral).

Dean further states, "A well-managed classroom is where students are engaged in their work, know what is expected, little time is wasted, the climate is work-oriented and pleasant, and learning occurs. The number one problem in the classroom is not discipline; it is the lack of procedures and routines" (amie@amiedean.com).

Behavior is communication, interaction, and perception. Perception is as powerful as reality; it is not what is said but what is heard. Behavior is learned over time and takes time and effort to change. Behavior serves to get something or avoid something. We all know that students choose their behavior, have a need to belong, and misbehave to achieve *attention* (annoyed), *power* (defeated/threatened), *revenge* (humiliated), or *detachment* (low self-esteem). Teachers who focus on showing students the correct behavior increase students':

- ✓ Self-esteem and pride
- ✓ Value
- ✓ Confidence
- ✓ Ability to learn to be responsible
- ✓ Level of care and compassion
- ✓ Problem-solving and risk-taking behaviors
- ✓ Ability to take the initiative to change incorrect behavior and learn from mistakes

Teachers will agree that once a classroom management plan is established, in place, and understood by the students, learning happens. Five-star teachers begin every school year by explaining to the students the positive procedures, rules, and processes including schoolwide established consequences. Most teachers will agree that consistency is the most difficult factor of any form of discipline. Students watch everything teachers do and how they either react or respond to a situation.

Positive discipline is responsive discipline. It focuses on a sensation of great physical, social, emotional, and intellectual health. Teachers demonstrate how to manage your:

- *Emotions. Don't REACT.* Respond to students.
- *Time.* Manage it effectively.
- *Priorities.* Focus on balance.
- *Energies.* Take care of YOU.
- *Words.* Think before you speak.
- *Stress.* Have stress relievers in your life (Chapter 8).
- *Personal life.* Make this your #1 priority.

Positive responsive behavior systems include:

✓ *Steps for success.* Teach students how to be successful and obtain positive results. Discuss what success looks like, how it is achieved, and what the correct behavior feels like (not a system of checks and balances or detention slips).

✓ A *climate of care and compassion.* Continually emphasize that kindness and compassion will get you much further in life than cruelty and bullying.

✓ Teachers should be student advocates, showing them the correct way of doing things and modeling successful actions.

✓ *Reinforce to students that the behavior is not acceptable yet the student is valued.* We all make mistakes.

✓ Implement a schoolwide philosophy so students are not confused if they are traveling from one class to another with a different set of expectations from each teacher.

✓ Provide a list of what "to do," not "do not's." When given a list of "do not's," disconnected students attempt to see how many they can "do" and not get caught. Additionally, the list usually grows longer throughout the school year.

✓ Many of the attributes of the response to intervention (RTI) model that many schools have implemented successfully (www.rtinetwork. org) or the Positive Behavioral Intervention and Support model (www.pbis.org) that is equally successful.

The bottom line is that five-star teachers focus on understanding the students they teach and clarifying correct behaviors. Most often in a typical class, 75% of the students consistently follow the steps for success, 15–20% are fence sitters and can go either way on a given day, and 5–10% are chaotic and consistently challenge authority. Five-star schools don't make decisions based on 5–10% of the population. They create a climate where it is the right thing to choose the right behavior and response.

Top-chef teachers do the right thing and focus on what is real. They are there to help with the development of empathy, care, and compassion. All students need successful experiences, to be involved, and immediate

> **"**
> The teacher is the key catalyst in the motivational climate of the classroom. From the very first days of schooling, students begin to recognize and appreciate the fundamental differences in various teachers' approaches to motivation.
> **William Glasser**
> **""**

feedback. The key component of doing what is right and real is *behavior man-agement.* To F.E.E.D. students, there must be a schoolwide behavior management plan in place that everyone acknowledges, observes, and practices. If it is not schoolwide and everyone is doing their own thing, behavior will never change and a successful climate and culture will be nonexistent. There is an overabundance of research, books, and successful practices on building a schoolwide behavior management plan. The bottom line is for the principal with the administrative team to reinforce the norm of everyone on the same page with the same outcomes in dealing with the behavior of students. Unfortunately, the most consistent element in many schools is inconsistency.

A school that emphasizes positive behavior will have these characteristics:

- *Every student receives positive recognition at least three times (hopefully more) during the school year.* As mentioned in Chapter 2, our job is to find G.O.L.D. in every student who enters our building. It is very easy to be nice to someone who is nice and looks good. Realistically, we don't always have that but we are there to ensure that all students know what it feels like to be successful. The students who are the most difficult to love are usually the ones who need it the most.

- *There is a feeling of connectedness by the staff and students to the school.* In discussing commitment, pride, and purpose come into play. To reach students, you must be a connected part of the school, not just someone who shows up to give some lessons. And you must do what you can to make students and their families feel connected as well. Five-star schools plan many positive activities to help students succeed, highlight their talents, and make parents and communities proud. Connectedness is another "C" that is imperative in five-star schools.

- *Staff members are committed to respect the students and understand the community.* We have discussed commitment to a degree. Additionally, the commitment must spread into the homes and communities of our students. When I taught at Lacoochee, on one of our planning days at the beginning of school our principal implemented a fabulous activity. After a nourishing breakfast, he would load every adult who worked at the school on a bus. We would then ride the entire route of every student that attended our K–8 school. It reminded us of three things: (i) how "comfortable" school buses are, (ii) where are students came from, and (iii) how long some of our students were on a bus before arriving to our daily dos and don'ts. What a lesson.

- *Everyone actively participates in the workings of the school.* Five-star schools focus on teams as the most important way to make a positive impact. We are all in this together and we must work together to ensure success. This means that everyone is a member of a committee for the betterment of the school. It is all about WE rather than ME.

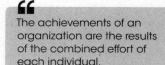

- *Positive public relations exist with the staff being the proudest communicators of goodwill.* To reach students, we *must* reach parents and community members. It does take an entire community to raise a student. Any attempt to share the great activities that are happening in the school is a step toward building relationships and positive public relations.

- *Care and compassion are the basis for all decisions made.* Again, we can't discuss this topic enough, especially today, when our students have so much to deal with through the internet, social media, celebrities, wanting to be noticed, and role models (positive AND negative). We have no control over their home lives, but we can control what happens when they enter the school.

- *Parents and community members are valued and invited to the school regularly.* If you have heard me speak you know that I always refer to the people who are E.A.G.L.E.S. (Enthusiasts Affecting Growth and Learning for Every Student) and who are D.U.C.K.S. (Depending Upon Criticizing and Killing Success). We know who they are. I believe there is at least one person who quacks on a daily basis (and most time he or she doesn't even realize they are the biggest D.U.C.K.) in every school. But the E.A.G.L.E.S. are the ones that F.E.E.D. students to make sure they don't S.T.A.R.V.E.

In my earlier book, I discussed how to deal with D.U.C.K.S. (page 103) and have expanded on the ideas:

- ✓ *Ignore the quacking.* Many times they want attention. Show them the want ads for supermarkets that need conflict-resolution personnel.

- ✓ *Confront the quacking.* Bring the person into a pleasant surrounding, offering coffee or a soft drink, and sit right next to her/him (not across a desk). After some small chat – just ask, "What would make you happier here?" If necessary, bring up specific incidents of quacking.

- ✓ *Attempt to see why they are quacking and so miserable.* The negative behavior may be a facade to conceal personal grief and sadness.

- ✓ *Assign them to a task.* Many times, D.U.C.K.S. feel unappreciated with unused talents. Find something they enjoy doing and attempt to capitalize on it through a schoolwide effort or club.

- ✓ *Talk privately to develop a positive plan of action* (especially if the toxic behavior is truly affecting colleagues and students). The severe cases where a D.U.C.K. is so negative that there are ongoing complaints, a one-on-one with the leader must occur.

✓ *Open up D.U.C.K. hunting season.* Give everyone duck calls to take to meetings. When a D.U.C.K. begins quacking with NO SOLUTIONS, everyone can blow on the duck call. Try to make the D.U.C.K. laugh.

✓ *Start an Adopt-a-D.U.C.K. program where you match an E.A.G.L.E. with a D.U.C.K.* When the negative person is having a *quack attack*, someone immediately get the E.A.G.L.E. to do D.U.C.K. control. Creating a buddy system does help.

✓ *Most importantly, do NOT let a D.U.C.K. take your day.* They will try. Be strong and supportive, but when all else fails, look them nose-to-nose and go "quack, quack, quack, quack," and walk away.

We must support students with behavior problems by teaching positive behaviors and skills for essential learning. We need to continually focus on student behaviors along with adult behaviors. Sometimes there are adults who need a course on effective behavior. When I do workshops with teachers on inappropriate behaviors, I ask them to list all of those behaviors of students. There is not one hesitation. Everyone is involved and states: unprepared for class, talking while I'm talking, cracking (southern term our kids use for yelling at others, put downs, sarcasm, etc.), out of seat, unorganized, note-sending, working on something else, cell phones, hoodies, gum, etc. The list goes on and on. I then love to attend a staff meeting and sit in the back of the room. I see every inappropriate behavior exhibited by the staff. To this day, I seriously don't understand why any adult would go to a meeting without a writing utensil and paper. It happens at every gathering.

We also need to know the difference between discipline and punishment. Discipline is firm and consistent but peaceful, whereas punishment damages self-esteem. We want to see a change in behavior with discipline but rarely do with punishment. Discipline takes time and energy and must be taught, but punishment is immediate. Lastly, discipline is not threatening or abusive but punishment can be emotionally and socially alarming.

Social Safety

No matter what grade level you teach, students are generally extremely social. They also begin to create their own social networks very early on. Teachers can tell the first weeks of school who are the social butterflies, who are the fence sitters, and who are the introverts. It doesn't take a genius. Social safety deals with well-being, acceptance of others, and sense of worth or value to self and others. Basically, it is one's self-esteem.

Five-star schools invest in building a positive social culture with a schoolwide focus on prevention and intervention. Nurturing and encouraging systems to teach positive social interactions and activities are ongoing. Time is taken to teach higher-order social skills to students to lessen the perva-

> **❝**
> You wouldn't worry so much about what other people thought if you realized how seldom they do.
> **Eleanor Roosevelt**
> **❞**

siveness of disruptive behavior. When teachers emphasize students' social needs, school environments are calmer and safer. In these climates, teachers can teach more efficiently, students learn better, students are contented and more engaging, the parents and community show a pride for the school, and life-long learning occurs for all.

If we can teach students at a very young age to develop positive social behaviors, to treat people with respect, to practice care and compassion, and to be nice, we will have fewer challenges in later grades. Teaching social skills begins the first days of school and continues to the last. Obviously, the ideal is to have the skills reinforced in the home and community.

Five-star teachers persistently help students know how to do things correctly. When inappropriate social behavior is demonstrated, teachers need to focus on the correct behavior. We want students to develop a positive image of self and uniqueness, knowing that there can be greatness in everyone. What can teachers do to help develop a positive social environment?

❖ Talk about self-esteem and effective ways to treat others with dignity and respect.

❖ Provide opportunities for social exchange and differentiated peer groups.

❖ Have ongoing "random acts of kindness" opportunities and make it the "in" thing for students to be kind to others.

❖ Have opportunities for students to talk about their concerns, stressors, problems, and challenges.

❖ Have a "safe room" where students know they have an adult they can talk openly and honestly to without fear or vengeance. If you are fortunate enough to have a guidance counselor at your school, this is something he or she can implement.

❖ Discuss what it means to be a good friend and have peer relationships.

❖ Promote visions boards and journaling.

❖ Model caring and teach students what it means to follow instructions.

❖ Use Post-it Note therapy (writing positive messages to students, colleagues, and parents on a Post-it Note and distributing daily)

❖ Try to mediate between social and academic concerns. A student who doesn't feel good about himself or herself is not apt to be on task academically.

Most importantly, be aware of the social issues in your school. Yes, with everything that is already on your plate, it is a lot to expect, but teaching is not an easy job. And take a hard look at the practices you are using to improve behavior, like in-school suspension, after-school detention, and out-of-school suspension (OSS has a detrimental effect to learning, and minorities are disproportionately affected). The US Department of Education published guidelines in 2014 to deter schools from using suspensions. Instead, focus disciplinary actions around new research-based models as positive behavioral interventions and supports (PBIS) and restorative justice (both used at MPMS). If we are not seeing an improvement in positive behavior, they are not working. We need something else. It takes extraordinary people to teach and make a difference in the lives of students. As Christa McAuliffe taught us, "You touch the future – you teach."

Emotional Safety

At every grade level, the emotional ups and downs of everyone in a school truly impact the overall success of the day. The five-star school strives to address all emotional barriers to focus on educating the whole child. We want our students to be emotionally safe and free from put-downs, sarcasm, bullying, and all negative actions that affect self-esteem. Students who feel emotionally safe strive to do their best and achieve at every level.

Peer problems impact the emotional safety of a student. Five-star teachers work effortlessly to ensure that students are taught how to be respectful to one another. Joe Coles recommends that to create emotional safety teachers must:

○ Teach the skills of resilience by teaching and practicing empathy.

○ Teach responsibility by encouraging contributions without fear of being made fun of or put down.

○ Teach decision-making and problem-solving skills so students can overcome peer conflicts and develop self-discipline.

○ Continually offer authentic encouragement and realistic feedback that helps students learn and improve.

○ Teach students how to make new friends and welcome new students to the school.

o Teach students that failure is not fatal and how to deal with mistakes and stress.

o Teach students the skills of effective listening.

o Teach students to be involved in their community.

For emotional safety to occur, the teachers must have a personal connection with every student they encounter. They have to be students' advocates and seen as individuals who enjoy their profession and working with students avoiding the use of sarcasm. Teachers need to model respect and dignity to all. Students know intuitively the teachers that don't want to be there. As Maya Angelou says, "If you know better, do better."

Another dynamic element is the social and emotional learning (SEL) movement for students, combining the two. We are critical players in building, consolidating, and emphasizing these competencies. Unfortunately, with all of the stress on teachers for Common Core Standards, ongoing testing, and teacher evaluations based on test scores, SEL has vanished and not been addressed adequately. One must understand and believe that without SEL it is very difficult to see high achievement. Students' social and emotional needs must be met first before they can achieve high standards. If a student is sitting in a classroom with no self-esteem, feeling irrelevant, and unworthy, she/he won't value the importance of learning and studying.

SEL will F.E.E.D. students. SEL is essential to promote in schools and classrooms. It helps students become kind, respectful, emotionally competent, and good human beings. When structured programs are implemented to help develop character and confidence, teachers and parents begin to see the development of the whole child. The premise of SEL is to help students develop good relationships with peers and adults and learn how to respect diversity and get along with others.

SEL involves the process to acquire and effectively apply the knowledge, qualities, and skills necessary to:

- Understand and manage emotions.

- Set and achieve positive goals.

- Feel and show empathy for others.

- Establish and maintain positive relationships.

- Make responsible decisions.

SEL helps us classify what is going on in our head and our heart. In the *art* and *heart* of teaching where social learning activates and involves the heart, emotional learning motivates and inspires the heart, and intellectual learning educates and informs the heart.

> Always be kind. If you see someone falling behind, walk beside them. If someone is being ignored, find a way to include them. If someone has been knocked down, lift them up. Always remind people of their worth. Be who you needed when you were going through hard times. Just one small act of kindness could mean the world to someone.
>
> **Author unknown**

Intellectual Safety

Obviously, we also want our students to be intellectually safe. Teachers in five-star schools know their students, their capabilities, their strengths, their challenges, and their backgrounds. Intellectual safety means teachers are there to help students find success, improve academically, and feel safe sharing and contributing during class. The research clearly shows that "a student's ability to progress in school is directly related to how effective the teacher is," as stated by Michele Rhee in the movie *Waiting for Superman*.

Teachers create environments where the surroundings are pleasant, engagement is encouraged, and sarcasm or intimidation is unacceptable. Intellectual safety says to students, "Your input is valued." Teachers who create a culture of intellectual safety:

- ❖ Recognize and understand the characteristics of the age group they are teaching.

- ❖ Provide a variety of teaching strategies that are involving, interacting, interesting, and inviting.

- ❖ Inform students of high expectations, proper procedures, rules, and processes.

- ❖ Allow students choice and input in teaching strategies and practices.

- ❖ Provide immediate feedback to students with respect and dignity.

- ❖ Encourage everyone to participate and create a classroom where involvement is accepted and encouraged.

- ❖ Provide peer mentoring so students learn to appreciate one another and work together.

- ❖ Inspire students to think outside the lines and share opinions without reprisal.

- ❖ Provide challenges for students to take risks and demonstrate knowledge.

- ❖ Provide a variety of resources and tools to learn and comprehend information.

- ❖ Be flexible.

❖ Use grading as a positive learning experience and never as a threat or negative consequence.

❖ Believe that all students can learn and have potential.

❖ Listen genuinely to all students and communicate expectations.

❖ Discuss students' growth and needs with other teachers and counselors.

❖ Participate in any opportunities for professional development for growth and development. They are always learners.

❖ Recognize that learning takes time and every student is not as excited about your lesson as you are.

❖ Vary the pace of lessons and allow for movement.

❖ Integrate lessons to show relevance when possible; team with other teachers.

❖ Have fun with the students and instill in them a joy of learning.

❖ Integrate and encourage thinking into every lesson.

❖ Have students demonstrate learning in their most effective mode.

❖ Let students realize they can't possibly know everything there is to learn. It is all right to not always know an answer.

❖ Do whatever it takes to help students succeed.

❖ Celebrate success, milestones, and experiences with students in a memorable style.

Intellectual safety in five-star schools ensures that we help students flourish. Education is serious business, and top-chef teachers model that belief every class, every day, every year, every student. They F.E.E.D. the students so they don't S.T.A.R.V.E.

F.O.O.D (Fulfilling Opportunities Offered Daily) for Thought

The following identifies sites, activities, and ideas that can be implemented to provide a safe environment for all. The administrative team can identify a group of adults to review these ideas and select the top 5–10 to begin addressing:

- Go to the following sites for more information on bullying (*People* magazine, October 18, 2010):

  ✓ www.wiredsafety.org

✓ http://www.pacer.org/bullying

✓ www.whytry.org

✓ www.ikeepsafe.org

✓ www.thebullyproject.com

✓ www.cyberbully411.org

✓ www.values.com (The Foundation for a Better Life, where you can get fabulous posters for free)

- Start an adopt-a-student program. Jeanette Phillips, past president of the National Middle School Association (www.amle.org) and an extraordinary middle school principal in Fresno, California, for many years, implemented the following activities for her adopt-a-student program:

  - Choose one or more of your students who need extra attention.

  - Make daily eye contact. Avoidance skills are learned early; breaking it down takes time. You may make eye contact for a long time before it is reciprocated.

  - Make daily verbal contact with the student. Call the student by name and speak to him or her whenever you see him or her. There is no greater reinforcement than being recognized by name.

  - Greet the student positively and let him or her know that you are glad to see him or her. Say good-bye and I'll see you tomorrow when they leave. Attendance problems decrease when students feel like someone is looking forward to seeing him or her.

  - Provide tutoring when possible and ask the student if help is needed.

  - Encourage the student to go out for an extracurricular activity.

  - Watch who the student is spending time with and keep a mental record.

  - Attend a school activity in which the student participates. Try to let him or her know you are there and comment the next day.

  - Write praise and success cards and use "Post-it Note therapy" to help the student's self-esteem. Disconnected students usually lack confidence and need to experience success and recognition.

- Keep track of the grades and talk to him or her, or if the student is not in your class talk to his or her teacher.

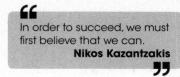

> In order to succeed, we must first believe that we can.
> **Nikos Kazantzakis**

- Be authentic. Students know when people are not real. Most importantly, be fair, caring, and sincerely concerned.

- Talk to the other teachers about the success of this student and encourage them to recognize the student also when possible.

- Match positive, sincere, fabulous students with your student so he or she can see what a difference a positive attitude and outlook can make.

- Encourage peer tutoring and mentoring experiences.

- Contact the student's parents or guardian when possible with positive comments. Try to involve parents and guardians as much as possible.

- Check attendance and office referrals. If your student is absent, phone home. Let him or her know that he or she was missed.

- If the student is absent, ask why and see if you can help with missed assignments.

- Give the student a responsibility. This can be any task that gives students ownership, gives power, and makes him or her feel relevant and needed.

- Pay sincere compliments and positively recognize the student every time possible.

• Establish a bullying prevention committee of teachers, students, parents, and community members that all agree to work together to end harassment.

• Discuss the behaviors that are most common and disruptive as a staff (i.e., cell phones, hoodies, hanging pants). Look at each infraction and determine a solution (no hoodies or parents are called). Let them use cell phones during lunch? Decide the swords you want to fall on.

• Have an outdoor supervision plan to monitor all activities on the school property.

- Have a variety of social activities for all students. Teach appropriate skills so students know the correct behavior in the lunchroom, at an assembly, at an event, or any other school activity.

- Use the resource officer to the maximum potential available.

- Create recipes for building a safe school environment and producing strong relationships.

- Learn from Principal Kafele by viewing his extraordinary videos and hearing his message: www.principalkafele.com.

- Have a variety of clubs and attempt to ensure every student is involved in some activity outside of the regular curriculum. If possible, use parents and community members to assist.

- Implement a plan for new students that matches him or her up with a positive peer mentor for the first week to ensure introductions to positive peer groups occur.

- Implement as many different and diverse opportunities as possible so all students can fit into a niche.

- Encourage students to create vision boards where they take a poster board and paste pictures, words, goals, and dreams everywhere, outlining their hope for the future. Have the students share and then display them for everyone to see.

- Encourage students to journal so they can write down feelings, frustrations, stressors, and how they will cope.

- Visit www.geniushour.com as a staff to learn your purpose and passion.

- At the beginning of the school year, have your class or team of students conduct a three-to-five-minute presentation on something they do exceptionally. It could be playing the violin to making a cheese sandwich. Of course each presentation must be preapproved, but it starts the school year off with a successful activity of choice with no losers and success for all. *Get to know your students* beginning the first day. Harry Wong's book *The First Days of School* is a useful tool.

- Teach students the skills of organizing, note taking, test taking, reading, writing, listening, speaking, visioning, risk taking, and communicating effectively. Make this an ongoing activity.

- Have each teacher shadow a student for a day – this works for all level pre-K to 12th grade (someone from the district office can be the substitute du jour). Nothing opens teachers' eyes wider than being a student for the day and seeing what they experience.

- Invite students and teachers to assess the climate by asking three questions: What do we need to keep on doing? Stop doing? And start doing? to become a safer five-star school.

- Discuss what a lack of motivation looks like and different techniques to motivate the unmotivated students.

- Have teachers discuss the following in small groups:

  - Students in this school misbehave for the following reasons:

  - Our top five behavior problems in priority order are:

  - Our current climate is:

  - To change inappropriate behavior teachers must collectively:

Share the thinking and begin an action plan to improve behavior.

- I always share my "qualities of a great person" checklist and questions to have staff complete and discuss:

  - The talent to care and be concerned for others (Do you CARE about YOU first?)

  - A desire to be successful (Define success.)

  - A feeling of good physical and emotional health (What do you do to stay/model healthy?)

  - The skill to think logically in all situations (Remember Bloom's Taxonomy? See Chapter 11 for a reminder.)

  - The capability to handle stress (What are your stressors, and how do you deal?)

  - The gift to have fun and laugh (Do you laugh at least once a day? At what? With whom?)

  - An attitude of gratitude (What are you thankful for?)

I then ask the adults to discuss in small groups the following questions to drill deeper:

1. On a scale of 1–10 with 10 being the best, on most days what would you rate your overall attitude?

   _____

   _____

2. On that same scale: where would you rate your attitude toward your job? Your colleagues? Your administration? Your students?

   _____

   _____

3. What do you do to maintain a positive attitude when things get tough?

   _____

   _____

4. How do you demonstrate to students that you genuinely care about each and every one of them?

   _____

   _____

5. What activities do you engage in to improve and/or adjust your attitude when you are feeling down?

   _____

   _____

6. How do you help students obtain/maintain positive attitudes?

   _____

   _____

7. What are three events that could transpire to improve your attitude toward students and work?

   _____

   _____

8. Do you *honestly* believe that *all* students can learn? Circle YES or NO. Provide supporting statements to your response:

   _____

   _____

- Have the staff answer the statements using the rating scale:

5 = Strongly agree; 4 = Agree; 3 = Undecided;
2 = Disagree; 1 = Strongly disagree

STATEMENT	RATING
1. Our school is a fabulous place to work.	_____
2. I know the mission, vision, and core values of our school.	_____
3. I have a positive attitude MOST of the time.	_____
4. I LOVE my job.	_____
5. I model respect and dignity daily.	_____
6. I respect ALL of my colleagues.	_____
7. I respect ALL of the students.	_____
8. I have trust and respect for the administration.	_____
9. I feel free to tell my principal anything.	_____
10. I am a POSITIVE AMBASSADOR for our school.	_____

- Encourage everyone to keep "gratitude journals" expressing everything they are grateful for in their life.

- Design the cafeteria to represent a positive culture and healthy choices with positive sayings everywhere, centerpieces (donated by local groups), and any other essentials that make students feel special.

- Have a "what do you do well" week at the beginning of the school year where students in their teams/classes show the adults something they do well (approved prior to the presentation and open to anything).

- Have a wellness club for students and adults.

- http://www.youtube.com/watch?v=iMSbypQnWgo: view the video as a staff and discuss.

- Show appreciation to staff and students in unexpected ways at unexpected times.

- Have a "Quit quacking" jar in the teacher's lounge (D.U.C.K. pond) where one must put money when they are caught quacking without providing a solution. Use this money for student incentives.

- Have a "discussion topic" at *every* staff meeting to get the staff to talk together and share. Include the topics equity, racism, sexual identify (there are students struggling with this and nowhere to turn), bullying, respect, and safety.

- Have a "meet and movie" activity where the staff get together, eat, and watch the movie *Gifted Hands: The Ben Carson story*, the Ron Clark story *Dead Poets Society*, the Erin Gruell movie *Freedom Writers*, or any other inspirational movie about the difference teachers can make.

- Discuss ideas and strategies to use when engaging the disengaged student: "What works for you?"

- Discuss a logical consequence and illogical consequence for each misbehavior (add more):

  ✓ Chewing gun

  ✓ No name on paper

SEVEN ACTIONS

MY BEST TEACHERS DID TO F.E.E.D.

1. Encouraged me.

2. Always willing to help me.

3. Guided me down the right path.

4. Stayed positive.

5. Made learning fun.

6. Has a good attitude.

7. Wants to see me do good.

By   Germaine, 10th grade

★MENU★

✓ Entering class late and disrupting learning

✓ Having no materials (pencil, paper, text, etc.)

✓ Hitting another student

✓ Verbally bullying another students

> " Students are willing to behave properly if they understand the ramifications, are given choices, are surrounded by a climate of care, and never humiliated.
> **Neila A. Connors** "

Obviously, in a five-star restaurant, there are a variety of options and choices available. The same is in a five-star school that has a goal to F.E.E.D. every student so she/he doesn't S.T.A.R.V.E. The next chapter provides a menu of possibilities.

To Turn Your Dreams into Goals, Remember Your ABCs

A-VOID negative sources, people, places, things, and habits.

B-ELIEVE in yourself.

C-ONSIDER things from every angle.

D-ON'T give up and don't give in.

E-NJOY your life TODAY; yesterday is gone and tomorrow may never come.

F-AMILY and F-RIENDS are hidden treasures; seek them and enjoy their treasures.

G-IVE more than you planned to give.

H-ANG on to your dreams.

I-GNORE those who try to discourage you.

J-UST do it.

K-EEP on trying.

L-OVE yourself first and foremost.

M-AKE it happen.

N-EVER lie, cheat, or steal. Always strike a fair deal.

O-PEN your eyes and see things as they really are.

P-RACTICE makes perfect.

Q-UITTERS never win and WINNERS never quit.

R-EAD, study, and learn about everything important in your life.

S-TOP procrastinating.

T-AKE control of your own destiny.

U-NDERSTAND yourself in order to better understand others.

V-ISUALIZE it.

W-ANT it more than anything.

X-CCELERATE your efforts.

Y-OU are unique and no one can replace you.

Z-ERO in on your goal/target and go for it.

By Neila A. Connors

CHAPTER 4

Menu: A Variety of Options Based on Our Needs

Peppered with Choices and Salted by Positive Relationships

A great restaurant ensures that each diner is taken care of, that there are a variety of food options, and that individual needs/requests are met. When you visit a five-star restaurant, you are given many choices throughout the dining experience. Everyone taking care of you wants to make sure all of your personal needs are met. And most times while reviewing the menu, you realize how difficult it is to make a choice because there are so many tantalizing options. The same occurs in great schools. It must be our role and purpose to provide a variety of learning experiences, choices, and opportunities for each student.

Adults in five-star schools go above and beyond to guarantee that there are activities appropriate for all. They create an atmosphere that FUELS, ENGAGES, and EMPOWERS students to make choices. Choices are based on *relationships* and *relevance*. When students have choice, the teachers F.E.E.D. (Fuel, Engage, Empower Daily) them. But it begins with building positive relationships. Tara Brown states, "The research is clear: humans are literally 'hard-wired' with the desire and need to connect. We are social beings who thrive on healthy relationships. And yet, the importance of positive relationships in our schools is often overlooked."

Building Positive Relationships

The number-one priority in a five-star school is to work on building positive relationships with every student and colleague as much as possible. When positive relationships are built, top-chef teachers assist students in developing social and emotional skills and achieving successfully. Developing positive relationships has a substantial and lifelong influence on students' academic, social, and emotional lives. Students know when teachers care about their happiness and social/emotional life along with grades and assessment.

" Students don't care what you know until they know that you care.
Author unknown
"

As mentioned previously, relationships are based on *trust*, and when students trust the adults in their school they enjoy school more, look forward to attending school, and feel more FUELED, ENGAGED, and EMPOWERED DAILY in their learning. Patricia Phelan, Ann Locke Davidson, and Hanh Thanh Cao stated in their article "Speaking Up: Students' Perspectives on Schools" (1992), "Students are more likely to be emotionally and intellectually invested in the classes where they have positive relationships with their teachers." Positive and strong relationships between teachers and students impact learning and achievement. The relationships we build with students, families, and colleagues are the fundamentals of everything we do. Most importantly, these relationships must be built early rather than when a problem arises.

Thomas Sergiovanni stated, "Schooling is first and foremost about relationships between and among students and teachers and community building (which improves teaching and learning)." Building the classroom community is of the essence because we want our students to feel that they belong, have a voice, have commonalities with other students, and commit to shared values and ideals. This must happen during the first weeks of school to have a productive and passionate year.

First Days/Weeks/Month of School

From the first day of school, a happy environment must be presented. Spend the first days/weeks/month of school making your classroom inviting and warm and learning about your students (#1 GOAL). Doctors don't give a prescription without a physical. Absorb as much as possible about your students. The more we know, the better prepared we become. Let them know how much you love your job and how proud you are to be their teacher. Share some personal information with the students (pets, kids, talents, etc.).

Top-chef leaders have an optimistic attitude about being a teacher and truly *care* about the students. They see the glass half-full and include students in most decisions. Let the students brainstorm ways everyone can decorate the classroom (if not decorated yet). Involvement of students is so important in building confidence. We want to build students' academic development and socially and emotionally appropriate behaviors. The first days/weeks/month of school can make or break your year. The first goal is to get to know your students personally. Take the time for activities where students introduce themselves and share likes and dislikes.

Students must be taught classroom expectations from the beginning. Two major components of building relationships are motivation and behavior management (discussed in a Chapter 3). Both work together in developing responsibility and start from the first days of school. Strategies are based on the clientele or student demographics. Know where your students are coming from, their cultural background, family life, family involvement in their school life, and any other variables that give you a well-rounded information base. If the majority of students come from homes where positive discipline exists and the family believes in attaining a good education, your job can be easier. If it is the opposite, you have a lot of work to be done. The challenges, many teachers face, are the lack of skills taught at home and parent involvement.

Show students the classroom procedures and expectations. Procedures are expectations for student behavior. If they need to line up against the wall outside before entering class – show them how. Do it over and over again until they get it right. The same with the first activity they must do once in their seats. Again, you can't overstress your team's expectancies. Harry Wong in his fabulous book (*First Days of School*) states, "Student achievement at the end of the year is directly related to the degree which the teacher establishes good control of the classroom procedures in the first week/month of the school year." Take a school walk or have the key players of the school come into your classroom so students know who they are and their roles. We are there as student advocates and want to make them comfortable at the beginning of the year. Plato said, "It is how you begin that is the most important."

At our school, teachers are visible all of the time. At the beginning of class, they are at their doors (unless an emergency has happened) to observe the behaviors that are entering the classroom, and at the end of class they stand at the door to say have a great day. This small action is vitally important because it gives teachers a heads-up on the mood of the students entering the room and anything that may be about to erupt. As Harry Wong always said, "If possible, touch each student on their shoulder as they enter to give a personal touch. No one has ever gone to jail for shoulder touching." At our middle school, our kids are huggers. They fly right into you without warning. That indicates trust. Trust cannot be presumed; it must be earned. To *teach* the student you must *reach* the student.

At the beginning of school, these important veins of successful classroom behaviors need to be taught over and over and over again until the students master what is expected of them. As indicated, if there is a specific strategy to entering the classroom, getting out books and supplies, and beginning an "opener" or "bell ringer," students need to review and practice this expectation until mastered. The more time you spend on this at the beginning of the year, the better the year will progress.

Additionally, during the first days/weeks/month of school, communicate with as many parents as possible to start the year off on a positive note. If you start positively, parents are more likely to be involved down

> **"**
> Enthusiasm is the match that lights the candle of achievement.
> **William Arthur Ward**
> **"**

> I have come to the frightening conclusion that I am the decisive element. It is my personal approach that creates the climate. It is my daily mood that makes the weather. I possess tremendous power to make life miserable or joyous. I can be a tool of torture or an instrument of inspiration, I can humiliate or humor, hurt or heal. In all situations, it is my response that decides whether a crisis is escalated or de-escalated, and a person is humanized or de-humanized. If we treat people as they are, we make them worse. If we treat people as they ought to be, we help them become what they are capable of becoming.
>
> **Haim Ginott**

the road if something negative occurs. Be proactive and introduce your team to the parents. Reach out to parents immediately (with their designated communication means) if a conflict occurs. Also, be cautious when receiving a negative email or parent response. Be proactive and professional.

Seize the Day

Building positive relationships requires the teacher to *C's* the day (*carpe diem* – seize the day) through: *Connections, Commitment, Consistency, Choices, Challenges, Collaboration, Communication* (Chapter 7), and *Celebration*. Reviewing the C's provides ingredients for a top-chef teacher to F.E.E.D. the students.

Connections

To assist students in obtaining the desire to learn, we have an obligation to connect with them. The most vital factors in establishing *connections* are to learn students' names as soon as possible (learn the correct pronunciation); find out personal likes, interests, and goals; talk to students; and ask for input and feedback (Chapter 9). Students need to be involved to *connect*. When you connect with students, you show that you *care*, providing encouragement and support. Be an advocate for your students. Most people when remembering their favorite teachers remember those who truly cared, not because they mastered their subject matter. You have 1440 minutes in a day; what do you do with them? As noted in Chapter 1, "Students don't care how much you know until they know how much you care."

Commitment

Commitment is the cornerstone of enthusiasm. Teachers have commitment to themselves, to others, the students, colleagues, the principal, administrative team, and the profession. They develop a classroom environment that breathes motivation by focusing on the positive and creating an atmosphere of success. There is a commitment to high expectations and

> In the middle of a difficulty lies opportunity.
>
> **Albert Einstein**

teaching students the correct way to succeed. They listen carefully, integrate learning, show how to succeed, and model a code of ethics.

Five-star restaurants show an "above and beyond" commitment to the customers. Five-star schools do the same. When any leader is asked what the difference is between change that delivers results and initiatives that fall short, the response is most likely to be *commitment.* The indisputable commitment of those accountable for the achievement is what makes the difference. And that commitment takes time, trust, and talent.

As I stated in my earlier book, "We have all heard the scenario concerning a bacon and egg breakfast. The difference is the chicken contributes whereas the pig commits." Abraham Lincoln said:

> **"**
> Commitment is what transforms a promise into reality. It is the words that speak boldly of your intentions. And the actions which speak louder than the words. It is making the time when there is none. Coming through time after time after time, year after year after year. Commitment is the stuff character is made of; the power to change the face of things. It is the daily triumph of integrity over skepticism.
> **"**

The *stuff character is made of and the power to change the face of things –* consider the *potential* of that statement. Committed adults believe in students, focus on strengths, provide feedback, model effectiveness, and enjoy the profession. Again, caring relationships are the key to "*change the face of things.*"

A committed person can be recognized instantaneously, no matter what profession. A committed person believes in what he or she is doing, shows up consistently, spreads the good word, takes joy in accomplishments, and does not let roadblocks or setbacks suspend progress. Obstacles are seen as opportunities. Commitment is what converts a promise into reality and shows that your words speak boldly of your intentions. Commitment is the "stuff character is made of," loyalty, and the power to strive to be the best. It is the daily conquest of reliability over doubt.

Consistency

The most difficult behavior to demonstrate in life, work, and schools is consistency. Yet it is so important especially in schools because students watch everything we do and they recognize inconsistencies. Consistency helps students learn the procedures, rituals, rules, and expectations. Consistency provides a foundation for learning. Consistency is the way five-star schools and teachers do things. The time is always right to do what is right. The schoolwide team agrees on practices, rituals, regimes, and acceptable behaviors. We all have the *struggle to juggle* with so much on our plate and so many new recipes coming in from all sections; learn to manage your time, seek balance, and avoid procrastination.

A simplistic example of inconsistency was demonstrated when I was visiting a middle school. I approached a student and was asking him about the school. I asked about the rules, and he said, "It is very confusing here. If you're chewing gum in Mr. ____'s class he says, 'Throw it in the garbage.' If you're chewing gum is Mrs. _____'s class, she says, 'Go to the office.' But if you're chewing gum in Mrs. ____'s class, she says, 'Great, do you have an extra piece?'" As trite as that may sound, there are still some schools that argue over the gum-chewing rule, and having inconsistent rules of any sort is a sign of a confused school that makes its "customers" uncomfortable.

In a reliable five-star school, all the adults and the students in the building consistently recognize the systems and procedures and stand by them. Consistency is obtained through effective, ongoing, and positive communication.

Choices

When you truly care about being successful, a top-chef teacher provides students with choices in behavior, academics, relationships, and how to be successful. The top-chef teacher provides a variety of strategies including direct instruction, students working together, reflection, and self-assessment. Students are given choices in how to complete assignments, consequences, and other aspects of daily situations. We need to teach students to "always remember you are braver than you believe, stronger than you seem, and smarter than you think." (You can find this, not in A. A. Milne's stories of Christopher Robin, but in Disney's 1997 video *Pooh's Grand Adventure: The Search for Christopher Robin*.)

All adults and students are faced with choices and on a daily basis. Hopefully, through our commitment to being a five-star school, we will make the correct choice and observe challenges as opportunities rather than obstacles. Maya Angelou said, "I did then what I knew how to do. Now that I know better, I do better." We must teach this to all members of the school community.

Our choices are based on our *attitude*. And our attitude is based on the buffet of choices we are given every day. The most important aspect of attitude and dealing with choices and challenges is that you must realize you *cannot stress* over that which you have no control.

Challenges

> **"**
> I have no special talents. I am only PASSIONATELY curious.
> **Albert Einstein**
> **"**

So many challenges in teaching. It is amazing how many situations you deal with on a daily basis that have no correlation to instruction and academic. Drama in schools today is predominant, and the social media has added an extreme supplement to all educators' plates. Attempting to cover all of the curriculum while trying to be creative and include guided practice, projects, direct instruction, rubrics, group instruction, while building the suitable groundwork is mind boggling. Turn challenges into opportunities. Strive for perseverance, positivity, purpose, and persistence. We want to create tenacious students ready to take on the world and become first-class citizens. To accomplish that feat, we must understand the attitudes and dispositions that the students bring to the classroom and work collaboratively to build learning environments, activities, and curriculums that include ALL students.

> **❝**
> Better teaching never comes from a political mandate. It comes from the heart of a prepared and caring teacher.
> **Robert John Meehan**
> **❞**

Collaboration

As stated in a previous chapter, teamwork is essential in creating a motivating structure. Working together with colleagues can help you learn other techniques and strategies, and work simultaneously in finding success for difficult students. Also teaching students how to be a team member and work together is essential. All participants are valued, and there is a strong sense of purpose. Collaboration requires high trust and a sense of shared responsibility.

Communication

Communication is the key to success in effective schools. I believe if the principal and administrative team worked thoroughly on developing a transparent and sure-fire system of communication, many challenges would be minimized (Chapter 7).

Celebrations

When students learn how to recognize self-worth, a sense of competence, and self-discipline, it is time to celebrate. Students are different now. We cannot employ the same methods and techniques used years ago before technology. Diversity, variety, recognizing prior knowledge, while relating learning to real life are the real motivating factors. We have to give students a reason to want to learn.

Many sit in classes and question why they need to learn something, and unfortunately our response many times is "to pass your statewide test in April." Celebrations must be ongoing in FIVE STAR SCHOOLS. We begin by celebrating diversity, by displaying posters, paintings, and portfolios of famous individuals in history who have the same background, traits, and languages as our students. We then celebrate the students who respect one another, the adults, being kind, on task, respectful, and mindful and applaud them. You celebrate by having an:

"L" of a day, every day, by:

✓ Living (a full and exciting life) to the fullest

✓ Learning (something new every day)

✓ Loving (yourself, your family/friends, and your professions)

✓ Laughing (EVERY day; a day without laughing is a day without sunshine)

Celebrate life and what you have been given. Life is short so enjoy each day to the fullest. Once you "C's" the day, you tackle relevance.

Relevance

Education is not just planning for college – it must be realistic. The focus on relevance is needed for students to embrace learning and understand the purpose of what they are absorbing. Education author Saga Briggs stated in *How to Make Learning Relevant to Your Students (and Why It's Crucial to Their Success)*:

> **66**
> We've all heard our students ask the question, When will I ever use this in the real world? And honestly, it's a great question – one that we should all spend more time thinking about. Research shows that relevant learning means effective learning, and that alone should be enough to get us rethinking our lesson plans. The old drill-and-kill method is neurologically useless, as it turns out. Relevant, meaningful activities that both engage students emotionally and connect with what they already know are what help build neural connections and long-term memory storage. **99**

Along with ENGAGE, they FUEL and EMPOWER students.

Briggs further stated, "Students need a personal connection to the material, whether that's through engaging them emotionally or connecting the new information with previously acquired knowledge. Without that, students may not only disengage and quickly forget, but they may also lose the motivation to try."

When we demonstrate to students the purpose of the learning, other than to pass a test, we are teaching relevance. We look back at the taxonomy and take them from the acquire knowledge phase, to apply knowledge, to integrate knowledge, to real-world practices. Our final goal is for students to confront real-world complications and find resolutions individually or as a team. We use the strategies of brainstorming, guided practice, think-pair-share, cooperative learning, demonstration, reflection, questioning, short

> **NEVER** in the history of calming down has anyone ever calmed down by being told to calm down.
> **Author unknown**

lectures, graphic organizers, projects, presentations, problem-based learning, role-playing, note taking, and more.

Teachers who show students the relevance of their learning *fuel* them by getting them excited, engage them by asking how they see the learning as relevant, and empower them to discuss and imagine how this learning can be used in the real world. Through interdisciplinary instruction within teams, teachers can brainstorm ideas and collaboratively teach which impacts students' learning profoundly.

Again, the variety in procedures help F.E.E.D. the students repeatedly. Our goal is to help students constructively manage their social well-being and their emotional health. When our students witness the association between the insight to be increased and their personal life, learning occurs.

F.O.O.D (Fulfilling Opportunities Offered Daily) for Thought

The following ideas and activities will reinforce the importance of options and choices.

- ✓ Discuss with the staff ways in which you can build trust within students – what are your recipes?

- ✓ Discuss ways that you FUEL, EMPOWER, and ENGAGE students daily in your classrooms.

- ✓ Purchase the book *Success Habits – A Student's Guide to Succeeding in School, Work & Life* by Rockell Bartoli for every adult. Have a special "get-together" to discuss the habits being used by teams and what should be included and improved.

- ✓ Discuss what barriers to trust exist in your school. On your team. In the classroom. How can they be turned into positive opportunities?

- ✓ Have teams review this outstanding message that is written for all to see. Challenge them to come up with their own team message (or you can do this with the entire staff):

> Human beings, like plants, grown in the soil of acceptance, not in the atmosphere of rejection.
> **Author unknown**

The sign written inside this fabulous restaurant in Connecticut

Welcome to

★ **Burton's** ★
Grill and Bar
of South Windsor

where we pride ourselves on offering you a professional, individual, and sincere dining experience. Our food is fresh and flavorful, always prepared from only the highest quality ingredients reflecting our chef's SPIRIT and your special requests.

We welcome the opportunity to create a unique culinary and service experience for you and your guests. If you're craving something special, feel like settling in for a while or have only a short time before your next engagement – let us know. We can MAKE THAT HAPPEN!

✓ Examine why you chose teaching as your profession and what challenges you face daily.

✓ Teams can develop a list of strategies to develop positive adult–student relationships. Share as a staff so everyone can prepare their own cookbook.

✓ Provide mini "how-to" presentations to staff on topics of their choice to help them improve.

✓ Remind staff of the following chart. Review and discuss:

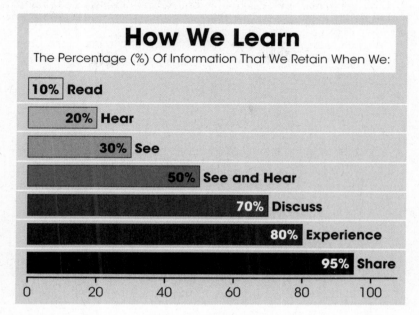

How We Learn

The Percentage (%) Of Information That We Retain When We:

10%	Read
20%	Hear
30%	See
50%	See and Hear
70%	Discuss
80%	Experience
95%	Share

0   20   40   60   80   100

✓ Develop a list of strategies to successfully motivate students. What is working and what is not?

✓ Develop a schoolwide code of ethics.

✓ Purchase every staff member a copy of Harry Wong's book *First Days of School* to distribute during pre-planning. Discuss some of the excellent elements.

✓ As a team, review the strategies of brainstorming, guided practice, think-pair-share, cooperative learning, demonstration, reflection, questioning, short lectures, graphic organizers, projects, presentations, problem-based learning, role playing, and note taking. Discuss the techniques you use, some you want to try, and some that are not included that you have found successful. Share this schoolwide.

✓ Discuss how you promote social and emotional learning in your classroom. Provide specific examples and what works most effectively.

✓ Each team lists every student on their team on a sheet of paper. Each teacher writes three positive statements about each student, a personal learning, her/his learning style, and a challenge. Have a team meeting to compare notes and discuss. Keep these notes in the students' team folders.

✓ Develop a program for staff and students accentuating social and emotional learning so school is a nurturing place where relationships are strong and nourished.

✓ Provide students with *shake breaks* where they can take a minute to stand, refocus, and shake it off. Possibly play some music during this time.

✓ *Have students complete this form:*

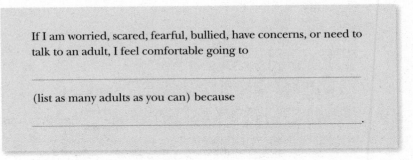

> If I am worried, scared, fearful, bullied, have concerns, or need to talk to an adult, I feel comfortable going to
>
> _____
>
> (list as many adults as you can) because
>
> _____.

We really need to look at this information, especially for the students who don't list anyone.

✓ Provide students with mini-workshops on how to be a team member, how to work collaboratively, and how to become self-disciplined.

✓ Always have extra activities for students who finish their work early.

✓ Allow students to teach the lesson when possible. Students love to write on the smart board or white board. Teach them to act like a teacher and take the role seriously.

✓ Suggest ways in which staff can give students choice and control over their assignments so they can connect with their learning style.

✓ Let students generate a list of what would motivate them to do better in school (realistically). Then list what demotivates them.

In the next chapter, we can show how we F.E.E.D. students by providing an administrative team who values students and all of the adults in the school.

The mediocre teacher tells,

The good teacher explains,

The superior teacher demonstrates,

The GREAT teacher inspires.

Author unknown

> **"**
> What a child feels about self determines what and to what degree anything is learned. May every child be given the essence and dignity of self by one caring and giving teacher. For it is of this sowing that the harvest comes.
> **Bob Stanish, *The Giving Book*
> 🍓**

SEVEN ACTIONS

MY BEST TEACHERS DID TO F.E.E.D

1. Mrs. Reynolds – Be happy and SMILE!

2. Ms. Gaye – Follow directions.

3. Mrs. Odom – Don't worry about what others say.

4. Mrs. Godwin – Sit down and be quiet.

5. Mrs. Butler – Learn to laugh and have fun.

6. Ms. Stephens – Learn to think for yourself.

7. Mrs. Kendrick (Grandma) – Have confidence and be proud of who you are.

By | Ebony Christmas, 10th grade

Average

I don't cause teachers trouble, My grades have been ok.

I listen in my classes, And I'm in school every day.

My teachers say I'm average, My parents think so, too.

I wish I did not know that, Cause there's lots that I'd like to do.

I'd like to build a rocket, I've a book that tells you how,

And start a stamp collection, Well no use trying now.

Cause since I found I'm AVERAGE, I'm just smart enough to see,

It means there's nothing special, That I expect of me.

Nobody ever sees me, because I'm in between,

Those two standard deviations, on each side of the mean.

I'm part of the majority, that "hump" part of the bell,

Who spends his life unnoticed, in an average kind of hell.

Good habits formed at youth make all the difference.

Aristotle

CHAPTER 5

"This Way, Please": An Effective Leader and Vision

Effective Leadership Is the Key to Success

Five-star restaurants have exceptional managers and assistant managers that expect the finest from everyone on their team. Extraordinary leadership is an important key to successful organizations. When you enter a five-star restaurants the first person that greets you is the hostess. She/he welcomes you and is attentive until your needs are met and you have been seated. You will see the managers throughout the experience getting involved, helping when necessary, and making sure everyone's experience is top notch.

In five-star restaurants, the manager/leader is visible and aware of the surroundings. Sometimes she/he even checks on your well-being and asks if anything is needed. The manager/leader is the one who has met with the staff prior to the opening, double-checked with everyone, and is noticeable throughout your meal to answer questions and assist whenever needed. Leaders of a five-star restaurants also do whatever it takes to make your dining experience seamless. They never ask you to do something that they wouldn't personally do.

In five-star schools, the front office manager is the hostess of the school. As discussed in Chapter 1, Mrs. Scott-Morrow is that person in our school. She goes above and beyond to welcome visitors into the building, assisting teachers and students while multitasking as she performs her countless duties. And she is always there to do whatever it takes to help students, staff, and parents with a smile.

Five-star schools are led by competent principals, assistant/vice principals, and deans building a functioning leadership team that also F.E.E.D. students so they don't S.T.A.R.V.E. As Susan Tardanico stated in her article "10 Traits of Courageous Leaders" (2013), "These are the times that call for bold, confident, courageous leadership. As history has shown, those with the guts to step forward, take some risks and lead change during downturns will be the winners as the economy rebounds." One of the main characteristics of high-performing schools is effective school leadership. Roland Barth shared, "If you are truly a leader, you will turn around and find others following you. If no one is there, you are just taking a walk."

Dennis Dempsey stated, "The most important attribute a principal needs to be successful is the right attitude. Five factors play a major role in creating this:

1. *Love kids.* Show kids you love them (F.E.E.D. them) and all decisions made will lead your heart in the right direction.

2. *Be a positive communicator.* Keep your community informed about what is going on in the school while being an extraordinary listener. Spend as much time listening as talking and be positive and passionate.

3. *Have a vision.* You must lead by example. If you believe you must lead your teachers and students to new concepts, technologies, and methods, you must do the same in your own work.

4. *Learn to fight the battles worth it.* Some battles just cannot be won. If the battle is worth it, make sure you do the preliminaries so that you can be successful in the long run.

5. *Have a sense of humor.* Laugh at yourself and laugh at situations over which you have not control. Learn to laugh with students, staff, and parents. It may be the one thing that will make or break your attitude and in turn your success as an administrator."

Scott Paulin ("Sharing the Journey," 2019) shared:

❝
The other thing to realize is that, as an administrator, you see everything that is broken or in need of improvement on the macro level, so it is easy to feel like things are going poorly. The reality, however, is that as you and your team address issues and head off problems proactively, you often find teachers saying things like 'that was a really good start of the year.' And you think, wow, it felt really rough to me. This is because you are dealing with all the rough edges so teachers can feel like it went smoothly. Administrators are the ultimate cat herders, jello-nailers, plate spinners – often feeling like you have a target on your front and tire tracks on your back – but if you lean into this and take on a servant-leader attitude, you can become the force that frees teachers up to teach and makes the whole school work. Roll up your sleeves, embrace the new chaos, and roll around in the messy joy of school administration. And remember to give yourself some grace. As a school administrator, there will always be more to do than can possibly be done. Eat this elephant one bite at a time.
❞

I could not have said it better. So true and relevant.

The primary goal of an active leader is to make lemons (difficult situations, circumstances, and experiences) into lemonade. Before a leader can become a L.E.M.O.N.A.D.E. leader and continuously F.E.E.D. students they must begin with a *vision, mission,* and set of *core values* developed, adopted, and practiced by all. The *head* and the *heart* of an organization are the *vision* and *mission.*

Vision

Great schools are great because of a leader with a vision (the *head* of the organization) that is ongoing and meets the needs of a changing world and involves collaboration by all. As Jonathan Swift stated, "Vision is the art of seeing things invisible." The vision is inspiration and short and simple. The essence of what you believe. The vision is what you ideally *want* to become. John Maxwell said, "The more you invest in the vision, the more it becomes your OWN." This vision is known and respected by everyone in the building and is usually a sentence or short paragraph providing a broad ambitious image of the future. Years ago, I worked as a consultant at Ocoee Middle School in Orange County, Florida. The vision was "Ocoee Middle School where the BEST get BETTER." It was stated everywhere in the building, and even when calling the school the secretary answered by stating the vision. There was no doubt as to the purpose and direction at Ocoee Middle School. The vision of MPMS is simply but powerfully stated: "*Success, Nothing Less.*" Dr. Witherspoon cites the vision during the morning announcements every day.

Mission

Once a vision is established, a mission statement evolves. A mission statement (the HEART of the organization) is relevant and creditable with input from all. The mission of the organization turns mirrors into windows. An organization without a mission statement is like someone taking a long journey with no map, direction, or knowledge of the final destination. Organizations that have a mission have a foundation and a belief system upon which every decision is based. Also, the mission statement is one that is known and "recitable," not written in a handbook with long words and sentences that no one can remember. The mission of the school is written to reflect the purpose, core values, identity, and aims. It is

> ❝
> Human relations include the most important words:
> SIX: I admit I made a mistake.
> Five: You did a great job!
> Four: What is your opinion?
> Three: If you please . . .
> Two: Thank you.
> One: WE
> **author unknown**
> ❞

the school's reason for being and provides a clear sense of direction around which goals and objectives can be established.

MPMS's is, "Our mission is to provide a productive learning environment where each student can recognize and maximize their learning environment." An extraordinary teacher, Mr. Neal Ford, who teams with me, starts off most classes by reciting the mission and reminding students of his purpose. And the core values are the lifeline that makes it all materialize.

Values

A set of core values is the lifeline that make vision and mission all materialize. Employees of the Red Robin restaurant chain, which has *fabulous food* and *fabulous service,* wear their core values on their sleeves – literally. Simply stated, they are "HONOR, INTEGRITY, SEEKING KNOWLEDGE, and FUN." Jokingly, an employee that I was talking with recently said that they are designed so you can turn the FUN comment under if you are having a bad day. Yes, I am also a realist – we all have bad or stressful days, which we will talk about later.

Great schools have values that are similar to Red Robin's. In organizations where care and compassion exist, one sees honor. *HONOR* is the pride inside that one feels and displays. Adults must be proud to be in a profession where they "touch the future – they teach" (Christa McAuliffe). This pride is demonstrated through words, actions, and encouragement. With honor follows truth. And we all know the truth will set you free. Always be honest with yourself and others.

INTEGRITY is the essential ingredient of soundness, morality, and success. Integrity is not only what we do or what we say but what we say we do – our internal representation of our self. Without integrity, there is no truth. I had the valued pleasure of working with a friend, mentor, and leader Jim Hoffmann in a business partnership (Educational Partnerships Incorporated). Our team has always said that Jim epitomizes integrity because he walks it, he talks it, and he lives it in everything he does. He never makes a major decision without discussing it with others, talking it through, looking at alternatives, analyzing how it will impact the organization (and

> ❝
> It takes all of us, for the woods would be very silent if no birds sang except the best.
> **Henry Van Dyke**
> ❞

the major players), being transparent, and focusing on a win–win philosophy. And everyone *trusts* him. Trust is a major facet of integrity. Without trust, there is no growth. Building trust demonstrates that the leaders are working for everyone's interests and there is never a hidden agenda. Trust is the ingredient of integrity that builds confidence in all.

SEEKING KNOWLEDGE correlates with life-long learning strategies. Every adult in an effective "five-star" school is continuously seeking knowledge about colleagues, students, parents, promising practices, new trends, research, community, and how to improve. A knowledge-seeker has the fire in the belly – the love of the job. And we know *"you can't burn out if you've never been on fire!"*

When you go to a Red Robin restaurant, you will witness the core value of *having fun* throughout your entire time spent there. It is a happy place for all ages, backgrounds, ethnicities, and belief systems, along with having a diverse menu. *Everyone* is welcomed and invited to have fun at Red Robin. There are balloons, smiles, singing, a mascot, and people who enjoy working there. Again, effective schools are places where people have *FUN*.

MPMS has the set of core values: *be respectful, be responsible, be ready*.

Each value is defined and on posters in every classroom and throughout the school.

Be Respectful

I can respect everyone's right to learn.

I can follow all directions.

I can respect all school property and materials.

Be Responsible

I can complete all assignments to the best of my ability.

I can place my cell phone out of sight and out of use.

I can bring all supplies to class.

Be Ready

I can listen to my teachers and peers when they are speaking.

I can always have needed class materials.

I can leave campus or report to assigned areas quickly.

> **"**
> Don't think about what can happen in a month. Don't think about what can happen in a year. Just focus on the 24 hours in front of you and do what you can to get closer to where you want to be.
> **By http://Hplyrikz.com**
> **"**

Once the foundation is established, the leadership team can F.E.E.D. students.

Their role is as important as the teachers' role. They FUEL students by knowing their names, their backgrounds, something personal about them, activities they are involved in, and encouraging them on a daily basis to be their best, respect the school and others, and to be appreciative for the ability to have a fabulous education with extraordinary teachers.

Leaders *engage* students by asking them questions, observing them in the learning environments, having them assist with school activities (doing the morning announcements), and being involved in decisions. They *engage*, according to Rudolf Dreikurs, "through *encouragement*, which increases students' confidence and builds self-esteem." Encouragement needs to:

- Build on strengths, not weaknesses.
- Work for improvement, not perfection.
- Comment on endeavors rather than results.
- View mistakes as efforts and not failures.
- Integrate students into the classroom community.
- Encourage, not just praise.
- Help students develop the courage to be imperfect.
- Show your acceptance of all students.

And they *empower* students when they give them choices, provide opportunities to explain situations about behavior and academics, and allow them to have some freedom. Leaders who F.E.E.D. students create a climate and culture that says to students, *"You are important and do matter to us."* Ultimately such leaders become L.E.M.O.N.A.D.E. leaders.

When Life Gives You Lemons, Become a L.E.M.O.N.A.D.E. Leader

Once the above is established, the principal and the leadership team can become L.E.M.O.N.A.D.E. leaders by exhibiting the following attributes:

*L = Learn, Listen, and Laugh with LOVE

*E = Enrich, Encourage, and Engage with Enthusiasm

*M = Mentor, Motivate, and Monitor with Meaning

*O = Observe, Oversee, and Offer with Optimism

*N = Nurture, Notice, and Navigate with Niceness

*A = Assess, Advise, and Appreciate with Authenticity

*D = Direct, Deviate, and Dare with Dependability

*E = Enthuse, Entrust, and Elevate with Eagerness

What does that really mean? Let's identify the ingredients in each component:

*L = *Learn, Listen, and Laugh with LOVE:* LL (L.E.M.O.N.A.D.E. LEADERS) learn something every day, listen more than they talk, and noticeably LOVE their job. Life is too short to be miserable.

*E = *Enrich, Encourage, and Engage with Enthusiasm:* LL are effective because they also F.E.E.D. the staff in the building with ENTHU-SIASM. They are the "cheerleader" leader encouraging the staff and not punishing the entire staff for the faults of a few.

*M = *Mentor, Motivate, and Monitor with Meaning:* LL are people others look to for mentoring and advice. They find purpose in the profession and assist adults when needed. They KNOW that everything in a FIVE STAR SCHOOL is based on successful RELATIONSHIPS with all of the adults and students in the building.

*O = *Observe, Oversee, and Offer with Optimism:* LL truly have vision that can assess the importance of our customers/students and optimistically look at every problem as a CHALLENGE. The quintessential challenge is to get extraordinary results. You must involve your TOP CHEF TEACHERS to make this happen.

*N = *Nurture, Notice, and Navigate with Niceness:* LL are the people who treat the staff with dignity and respect. They understand that successful schools happen because of successful leaders. They are NICE and have positive people skills.

*A = *Assess, Advise, and Appreciate with Authenticity:* LL recognize the POWER of appreciation and authentically care about everyone who enters the building. They ask for opinions, open up staff meetings

> **"**
> Extraordinary Leaders Put Their Heart into Their Profession:
> H: Hear and understand me.
> E: Even if you disagree, don't make me feel badly.
> A: Acknowledge the greatness within me.
> R: Remember to look for my *success* and *positive contributions.*
> T: Tell me the truth with compassion.
> **author unknown**
> **"**

for deep discussions, and appreciate what everyone does. I have always said, "The BEST leaders NEVER forgets what it is like to be a TEACHER, and the BEST teacher NEVER forgets what it is like to be a STUDENT."

D = Direct, Deviate, and Dare with Dependability: LL take risks. They color outside of the lines and go above and beyond the call of duty to ensure ALL staff and students are recognized and respected. LL do NOT have hidden agendas and lead by walking around and smiling. They SHOW UP physically and mentally daily and are seen visiting classrooms on a regular basis.

E = Enthuse, Entrust, and Elevate with Eagerness: LL also recognize the POWER of enthusiasm. They NEVER ask anyone to do anything that they would not do. They EAGERLY embrace the day and forge ahead with vigor and zest.

Effective leaders become better and *keep the fires burning* by initiating circumstances that augment the staff's *desire and eagerness* to direct energy toward attaining educational excellence through the planning and encouraging of participation, teamwork, and collegiality. They also support innovation, recognize and reward "top-chef" performance, provide ongoing feedback, serve as success coaches, and provide needed resources for all staff members and students. They are *visible* – seen everywhere throughout the school daily (hallways, classrooms, play areas, lunchrooms, restrooms, gymnasium, etc.) unless at a meeting or handling an emergency. The best principals walk into a classroom and no one acts amazed – it is a common activity.

One of the schools I worked in had a leadership team concerned about everyone. They instituted a "Friday Follow-Up Form" that was for staff members to complete on Friday. It was optional. They requested the following information.

Remember, plan to respond and *act* on the Friday Form in a timely fashion. When others see their responses are being addressed, more will complete the form. But remember: don't *ever* ask a question that you *do not* want to know the answer to. So, if you plan to implement a Friday Form, be prepared to act in a *timely* fashion on ALL questions asked.

Since extraordinary leadership is difficult to define, it is also problematic to directly quantify. Truly, leadership is about getting others to take action and stimulating the best efforts in others. It's the ability to motivate and make others feel like heroes.

> "
> Always be kind. If you see someone falling behind, walk beside them. If someone is being ignored, find a way to include them. If someone has been knocked down, lift them up. Always remind people of their worth. Be who you NEEDED when you were going through hard times. Just one small act of kindness could mean the world to someone.
> **http://Rachelschallenge.org**
> "

Name of staff member_____
Date_____

1. How was your week?

   _____
   _____

2. Did anything EXTRAORDINARY occur this week?

   _____
   _____

3. Is there a student (or more) that went above and beyond who you would like the leadership team to recognize? Please provide the name and the specific activity.

   _____
   _____

4. Any present concerns you have that you would like the leadership team to discuss?

   _____
   _____

5. Is there a staff member that you would like to recognize? Please provide her/his name and why.

   _____
   _____

6. Do you have any custodial, repair, or cleaning needs that you would like addressed?

   _____
   _____

7. Any additional comments:

   _____
   _____

F.O.O.D (Fulfilling Opportunities Offered Daily) for Thought

The following lists activities and ideas that the leadership team and staff can implement to create an environment where students don't S.T.A.R.V.E.

➤ Have a meeting to discuss what happens in the school to make it feel like "EVERYONE'S SCHOOL." Each team will discuss and then share. This activity can also be done with students.

➤ Conduct book studies for the staff three to four times per year where everyone votes on the book, a copy is bought for everyone, and a designated meeting is planned to discuss the contents. Chapters can be divided up for teams to present and a full discussion occurs. And you can actually fire up this with THIS BOOK. YES!

➤ Work with the entire staff to develop or refine the vision, the mission, and the set of core values. Ensure everyone has input.

➤ Have the leadership team and the staff (separately at first and then jointly) develop a vision board of where they want to be in one to three years (we know it takes three to five years for change to take place and be fully implemented).

➤ At a staff development session or meeting, ask teams to answer these three questions: what do we need to *keep* doing? What do we need to *stop* doing? and What do we need to *start* doing? The answers to these questions can begin a quest for quality. However, the leadership cannot ask these questions if they are not prepared to respond to the answers.

➤ Develop committees with students to discuss what needs to happen to make our school *extraordinary*. Have a regularly scheduled monthly meeting.

➤ With the administrative team, ask this question:

○ If you could get each of the professionals in your school to implement one or two strategies exceptionally, consistently, and would F.E.E.D.

students and influence their education progressively, what would that look like?

> Great leaders don't set out to be a leader. They set out to make a difference. It is never about the role, always about the goal.
> **Lisa Haisha**

➢ Have teams share with the staff ways in which they F.E.E.D. students daily. Put all the responses together and share at a meeting. Successful leaders share, share, share.

➢ Go to the site www.theenergybus.com by Jon Gordon and sign up for his positive weekly newsletter that has an overabundance of great ideas to implement when *feeding* students and one another.

➢ Have teachers individually complete a form that includes all the components included in their thoughts on "*best working conditions.*" Compile the list and discuss at a meeting.

➢ With the staff, discuss *leaders vs. managers* to have them realize they are the *leaders* in their classroom/teams and come up with their own descriptions:

- A manager administers; the leader innovates.

- A manager maintains; the leader develops.

- A manager relies on systems; the leader relies on people.

- A manager counts on controls; the leader counts on trust.

Once the leadership team models how to F.E.E.D. students (and teachers), it is up to the team of teachers to focus on the positive and help students achieve. An effective leadership team develops top-chef teachers. They are the individuals who work together and do whatever it takes to help students flourish and are extraordinary. Top-chef teachers F.E.E.D. students so they do not S.T.A.R.V.E.

TEN ACTIONS

MY BEST TEACHERS DID TO F.E.E.D. ME

1. Made learning easy.

2. Very understanding.

3. Did one on one work with me.

4. Always uplifted others.

5. Wasn't biased.

6. Didn't take anything from anybody.

7. Straight forward.

8. Cared about others' feelings.

9. Never judged anybody.

10. Was always positive.

To | Mrs. Wheeler
by | Chatanna Green, 10th grade

Recipe for High Staff Morale by Marion Payne
(outstanding retired middle
school principal and director)

- 1 pkg. Recognition

- 1 can Frequent Communication

- 1 cup Opportunity for Professional and Personal Growth

- Lots of Support

- Dash of Appreciation

- Pinch of Humor

  Mix together in a large container all the staff recognition that you can afford in 1 year with regular and frequent communication. Allow many opportunities for personal and professional growth. Top it all off with lots of support and appreciation sprinkled generously.

  Serve warmly. Garnish with pinch (or more) of humor.

CHAPTER 6

"I'll Be Your Server": A Team of Caring and Trained Adults

Caring and Compassionate Teachers Work Together to Provide Successful Experiences

In a five-star restaurant, once you have been seated the teamwork *begins*. You are provided service above and beyond with team members who work together, fill in for each other, keep everyone updated, and provide you with the type of service you crave. Someone is bringing you bread and a possible relish tray while others are filling your water glasses and taking your drink order. The top chefs, not cooks, are in the kitchen preparing elegant meals, and you feel as though you are the only customers in the building. Top chefs see their profession as a craft and possess a flair or magic touch. Whereas a cook does exactly what she/he is told and usually is not allowed to contribute creatively. Five-star restaurants do not have cooks: only top chefs. As your experience continues, timing is impeccable and you also value that you are truly receiving a five-star experience.

In a five-star school the teachers who F.E.E.D. students work together on a team and are the top chefs in the business. We need to have top-chef teachers in schools who truly like students and the profession. Just as a bad waiter or waitress can negatively impact an evening, a teacher can have the same effect on students. We have to first ask ourselves the question, why do we want to work in a school? If the answer is to make a difference for students, then we are in the right place. Teams are effective because it is the sharing of skills by several teachers who genuinely enjoy working together. They can sustain the enthusiasm and lend support to one another while motivating students. If you are in a setting where teaming is not possible, attempt to develop some projects or schoolwide activities where teams (randomly selected) can work together and present at a staff meeting.

When students are asked about their favorite teachers, in this day and age many respond with one word – *nice*. Yes, nice. Think about it. We all want

> **"**
> Teaming: Coming together is a beginning.
>   Keeping together is progress.
>   Working together is success!
>   **Source unknown**
> **"**

to be around NICE people. It is challenging to teach someone to be nice or care. It is an intrinsically developed behavior that comes naturally. And everyone knows who the *nice* people are in a school.

Caring and compassionate adults do whatever it takes to ensure success for all. Caring teachers recognize and take into account individual differences, diverse backgrounds, and when a student is just having a bad day. They don't practice the "never smile until after the holidays" adage and take the time to get to know all students – especially students who are the most unlovable. As in a five-star school, all "customers" are treated with the same respect. And the five-star treatment extends from the front of the building throughout the school into every nook and cranny.

The world's most successful chefs all have one attribute in common: an exceptional ability in the kitchen. Similarly, top-chef teachers have an incomparable ability in the classroom and working with students from ALL backgrounds and diversities. Top-chef teachers whip up delicious meals of excitement, involvement, and creativity on a day-to-day basis. They F.E.E.D. students so they don't S.T.A.R.V.E. without realizing how amazing they are and how effectively their skills challenge the minds of their students.

What does it take to be a top-chef teacher? The following will provide the most important ingredients you must incorporate into your life to be a top-chef teacher. Obviously, you will not demonstrate every characteristic every day because we are human and some days we are just pleased that we made it through the day. Do your best:

- *Ability to work successfully on a team (Together Everyone Achieves More).*
  I have been blessed to work with many schools as a consultant in all 50 states, Canada, and Europe. Truly, the most successful schools have the adults in the building teaming to any extent possible. When a school is fortunate to have a total group of top-chef teachers on a team, they focus on how to F.E.E.D. every student.

  Ideally, the team has the same group of students, meets regularly, discusses behavior management, develops strategies, and is consistent. A culture of collaboration is created through teams, and new teachers can learn how to become a top-chef teacher through mentoring and modeling. There is a plethora of research to support teaming and ways to become fruitful. The majority of the research proves that teaming positively influences student achievement, increases teacher satisfaction, builds relationships, supports the administration and a positive climate, increases parent communications, and builds consistency. TEAMING WORKS!

- *Resourceful organizational skills.* You must be prepared. Advanced preparation and planning is imperative and is key in becoming the best. Top-chef teachers are in high demand today, especially those who demonstrate a high quality of organization. As I said earlier, teachers today are inundated with so many mandates and expectations that it is vital to keep up with paperwork and requirements. Create folders for personal information, professional information, and student information. Everyone organizes her/his life differently, but it is important to find a system that works for you. I write everything on Post-it Notes, then lose them. That is NOT organization.

- *High expectations.* Start with high expectations of yourself. You can master anything that is given to you. Follow that with high expectations for all students and do your best to bring out their best. In the fabulous book *The Four Agreements* by Don Miguel Ruiz, he states, "You need a very strong will to adopt the FOUR AGREEMENTS:

  1. Be impeccable with your word.

  2. Don't take anything personally.

  3. Don't make assumptions.

  4. Always do your best."

- *Clear and focused communication.* In real estate, it is location, location, location. In our business, I firmly have confidence in communication, communication, communication. It is by far the most significant quality to have in schools to run smoothly and have everyone on the same page. Chapter 9 will thoroughly address the consequence of ongoing schoolwide, team, and overall communication.

- *Professional demeanor.* You show your self-respect by your professionalism. A professional attitude, philosophy, and overall appearance shows everyone that you have pride inside. Obviously, there will be dress-down days, but the way you act speaks volumes. You don't need to be your students' "friend" – they have enough and need positive and passionate role models.

- *Flexibility.* The most important word in education is the "F" word – flexibility. You *must* be flexible to be a top-chef teacher. Things are going to CHANGE, there will be upsets, people may disappoint you, but life goes on. Be as flexible as possible and your day/week goes so much better. Just go with the flow.

- *Willingness to accept disapproval.* Yes, there will be some students that don't

> **"**
> No one has ever drowned in sweat.
> **Lou Holtz**
> **"**

> **"**
> The first wealth is HEALTH.
> **Ralph Waldo Emerson**
> **"**

like you. Even some colleagues. Learn to love yourself so negativity does not eat you up. And if you receive a negative evaluation, learn from it. A top-chef teacher becomes better from growth and self-evaluation.

- *Clear understanding of students and their culture.* Know your students and their parents/guardians and home situations. If their culture is different than yours – learn it. Be respectful of where all the students come from. They did not choose their race, culture, parents, or situation. That was given to them. Do your ultimate best to learn as much as you can about every student. Again, this is where teaming is so vitally important because the team can work together to develop a plan to help any student that is having a difficult time learning, behaving, or just fitting into the system.

- *Openness.* A top-chef teacher must be open to her/himself, colleagues, and students. People know when you are not being authentic, are unhappy, and feel anxiety with your personal or professional life. Students also know when an adult doesn't like teaching or even kids. There are students who come up to me and actually say "Mrs. /Mr. _____really does not like us, we know." And they do. Talk to others. Speak during a staff meeting. Be open with your feelings, beliefs, and philosophies. If you have a concern, meet with the principal or leadership team.

- *Social and emotional intelligence.* A top-chef teacher has people skills and learns how to control emotions. Top-chef teachers do not get caught up in any form of screaming or irrational behavior. You can't let the kids "get your goat. The only way they can is if you let them know where you tied it." There are many social and emotional situations that can arise in any given day. At those times, breathe, count to a number, and think if this was MY CHILD, how would I want this to be handled. We can't ever embarrass or humiliate a student. Additionally, many schools have cameras everywhere and any action can be replayed in a minute. Treat others as THEY would like to be treated, in my opinion.

- *Ability to handle stress.* Everyone has stress in their lives. The only people who have no stress are no longer on earth. We need to worry about adult stress and student stress. This will be addressed thoroughly in Chapter 8.

- *A sense of humor.* A day without laughter is a day without living. There are so many funny instances and situations on a daily basis in schools – you *must* laugh. Again, because humor can F.E.E.D. students, Chapter 10 is dedicated to this topic.

As we work together, we become high-level functioning teams who work to be successful, have winning attitudes, continue to improve, assess continuously, and have FUN!

We also fill in for each other on "off" days. One person can be a crucial ingredient on a team but one person cannot make a team. And teamwork gives you the best opportunity to turn vision into reality where no problem is insurmountable. Courage, fortitude, and teamwork move top-chef teachers from ideas to action.

> " From an employee standpoint, a great place to work is one in which you trust the people you work FOR, have pride in what you DO, and enjoy the people you are working WITH!
>
> **by Robert Levering (A Great Place to Work)**
> "

F.O.O.D (Fulfilling Opportunities Offered Daily) for Thought

The following identifies specific activities and ideas to be implemented in producing effective teachers and staff:

> ➤ Have teachers identify the characteristics of a top-chef teacher.

> ➤ Ask teachers to review the following questions:

- • What does a high-functioning team look like?

- • How do we build trust on a team?

- • What is working? Not working? Need to start doing?

- • Do we have a clearly defined set of expectations on the team? Schoolwide?

- • What do we need to learn about teams?

- • How do we work together to become more consistent?

> ➤ Complete a survey on teaming, asking: Do I effectively work with others? Am I consistent? Do I communicate clearly and succinctly? Am I flexible? Do I enjoy working on a team? After everyone has completed answering these questions discuss each one and determine areas that need to be addressed.

> ➤ Have every team present at a faculty meeting three to five activities that have occurred recently and were done to F.E.E.D. a student to be successful.

> " People whose lives are affected by a decision need to be part of the decision-making process.
>
> **Source unknown**
> "

> No printed word nor spoken plea can teach young minds what they should be – Not all the books on all the shelves but what the teachers are themselves.
> **(author unknown)**

➤ Have teams/staff answer the following questions:

- ■ Do I communicate realistically with my team?

- ■ Do I cooperate and work toward being consistent with my team members?

- ■ Am I good with time?

- ■ Am I flexible?

- ■ Do I enjoy the students and have fun?

➤ Ask students to define "what a great team member" looks like and "what a great team" looks like.

➤ Have teams/staff review the stages of teaming to see where they are:

✓ The "polite" stage (I'm just so HAPPY to have a job.)

✓ The "where do I fit in" stage (Who are these people?)

✓ The "challenging" stage (power? Cliques? All as one?)

✓ The "bonding stage" (win–win; How can we improve?)

✓ The "esprit de corps" stage (We are family . . .)

➤ Have teams/staff review the barriers for teams to overcome and rate where you are as a team/staff:

- • Personality conflicts

- • Inconsistency

- • Poor planning

- • Time management

- • Lack of support for each other

- • Refusal to share ideas

- • Difficult member(s)

- • Inability to adjust delivery systems and strategies

- • Lack of honest communication and feedback

- • Does not BELIEVE in teaming

- • Poor people skills

- • Inadequate public relations

> Coming together is a beginning. Keeping together is progress. Working together is success.
> **Henry Ford**

➢ Have the teams decide on a book and complete a book study. Present the results at a staff meeting. An excellent book is *Deliberate Optimism* by Debbie Silver, Jack C. Berckemeyer, and Judith Baenen.

Once teams of caring and empathetic adults are in place we can then address the importance of communication in five-star schools. Our goal is for effective communication to be continuous.

TEN **ACTIONS**

MY BEST TEACHERS DID TO F.E.E.D. ME

1. Allowed me to express my feelings.

2. Made themselves available.

3. Was very positive.

4. Explained things deeply.

5. Cherished my ideas.

6. Always believed in me.

7. Expressed herself.

8. Gave me the opportunity to see how the world really is.

9. Put real live problems into my work.

10. Was never afraid to tell me when I'm wrong.

By   Lyric Stephens, 10th grade

For the Garden of Your Daily Living (source unknown)

Plant Three Rows of Peas
1. Peace of mind
2. Peace of heart
3. Peace of soul

Plant Four Rows of Squash
1. Squash gossip.
2. Squash indifference.
3. Squash grumbling.
4. Squash selfishness.

Plant Four Rows of Lettuce
1. Lettuce be faithful.
2. Lettuce be kind.
3. Lettuce be patient.
4. Lettuce truly respect one another.

No Garden Is Without Turnips
1. Turnip for meetings.
2. Turnip to help one another.
3. Turnip for students.

To Conclude Our Garden We Must Have Thyme
1. Thyme for yourself
2. Thyme for your family
3. Thyme for each other
4. Thyme for your friends

Water freely with patience and cultivate with love; you reap what you sow.

I Love Being a Teacher

I'm positively certain that I love just what I do.
I'm glad that I'm a teacher, a profession proud and true.
I try to go to school each day with a smile upon my face.
I respect all students' uniqueness, their culture and
their race.

N. A. Connors

★ Real Teachers ★

1. Will eat anything on a plate in the teacher's lounge.

2. Encourage the "quiet people" at a meeting to SHARE.

3. Always ask if anyone needs to use the restroom.

4. Raises their hand in a restaurant when the server asks if anyone wants water.

5. Tells kids in grocery stores to stop running.

6. PRAYS the "full moon" is on the weekend.

Lessons from the Geese – A Rationale for Teaming

As each goose flaps it's wings, it creates an "uplift" for the bird following. By flying in a "V" formation, the whole flock adds 71% more flying range than if each bird flew alone.

LESSON: People who share a common direction and sense of community can get where they are going faster and easier because they are traveling on the thrust of one another.

When a goose falls out of formation, it suddenly feels the drag and resistance of trying to fly alone and quickly gets back into formation to take advantage of the lifting power of the birds immediately in front.

LESSON: If we have as much sense as a goose, we will join in formations with those who are headed where we want to go.

When the lead goose gets tired, it rotates back into the formation and another goose flies at the point position.

LESSON: It pays to take turns doing the hard tasks and sharing leadership with people, as with geese – interdependent with one another.

The geese in formation honk from behind to encourage those up front to keep up their speed.

LESSON: We need to make sure our honking from behind is encouraging – not something less helpful (like quacking).

When a goose gets sick or wounded or shot down, two geese drop out of formation and follow their fellow member down to help provide protection. They stay with this member of the flock until he or she is able to fly again or dies. Then they launch out on their own with another formation or to catch up with their own flock.

LESSON: If we have as much sense as the geese, we will stand by each other like they do.

By Nerle W. Coos, editor ELCA

Those Who Can

Those who can – make failure bear fruit, bring fruit to seed, and plant seeds for tomorrow.

Those who can – turn injury to endurance, endurance to dreams, and give dreams substance.

Those who can – shape hate to awareness, awareness to grace, and crown grace with compassion.

Those who can – massage fear to faith, bend faith to courage, and sculpt courage into wings.

Those who can – subdue chaos with meaning, define meaning as light, and translate light to vision.

(continued)

Those who can – give knowledge reason, fashion reason into tools, and use tools as keys so that doors become opportunities.

Those who can – give charity character, invest character with strength, and free strength to ministry.

Those who can – define love by their acts, spin their acts to hope, and with hope give children a reason to celebrate.

Those who can – TEACH!

By Gavin Kayner

CHAPTER 7

Communication: Succinct, Effective, and Ongoing

The Key to Success Is Useful and Continual Communication

Five-star restaurants are the best because of one key element that is apparent throughout the entire dining experience – *communication*. Everyone who is a member of the team takes the time to communicate successfully with you so there are no misunderstandings from the beginning until the conclusion of the experience. The top chef sometimes walks about the restaurant intermittently to check on everyone, their meal, and confirm all is going satisfactorily.

I have always said that if we could come up with a plan to ensure seamless and transparent communication in schools, we would change the world. This is one of the most important elements yet continues to be lacking to some degree. Five-star schools work effortlessly to provide the best communication methods for all so everyone in the school is on the same page and the schoolwide team works as a well-greased machine. Everyone is using the same recipe. Effective communication is important for articulating feelings, concepts, and knowledge.

Continuing and regular communication will also F.E.E.D. the staff. We know that in real estate the key is location, location, location. I believe in effective organizations it is *communication, communication, communication*. Open, helpful, positive, and effective communication is crucial for schools to meet the needs of everyone. Obviously, it is the role of the leader (Chapter 4) to develop communication plans, networks, systems, boundaries, and procedures; but each person in the five-star school must contribute to the chain of communication or it can easily break down. I believe there is no such thing as *overcommunicating*. It is usually the lack of or inconsistent communication that causes stress, confusion, and incomplete actions. Our challenge is to F.E.E.D. students through modeling and teaching the tools to successfully communicate.

> **"**
> We are what we repeatedly do. Excellence then is not an act, but a habit.
> **Will Durant, *The Story of Philosophy***
> **"**

Our vast new communication world has made it easier to communicate but also sometimes overwhelming because there is so much to convey. Therefore, effective communication includes a filtering system to avoid trivia and unnecessary details. A system that is respectful and takes individual learning/communicating styles into effect is critical. George Bernard Shaw stated that "the single biggest problem in communication is the illusion that it has taken place." A friend and mentor, Dr. James P. Garvin, said, "Where there is effective communication, there is successful change. Change transpires one conversation at a time." So true. Growing organizations that meet the needs of clients are changing organizations that stay ahead of the curve. Thousands of books and articles have been written on communication.

Everyone will agree that *poor* communication is the basis for a large number of problems in schools and life. Our students need positive role models to show them how to be excellent listeners and speakers who have nourishing and valuable conversations. If this is not in their home, it is up to teachers to emphatically stress and teach this skill. Open lines of communication improve productivity, increase morale, and are the life blood of a five-star school. Communication supports the mission, vision, and core values of a five-star school. Communication in itself has a direct impact on performance at all levels.

In all the literature on communication, we learn that we absorb about 25% of what we HEAR and we communicate approximately 55% using our body language and 38% with the tone of our communication, and 7% of actual words said. And truly most of our communication is nonverbal, which includes body language, gestures, proximity, facial expressions, and eye contact. We spend roughly 40% of our time listening, 35% speaking, and 25% in a daze and not focused. On top of that, add all of the emails, newsletters, text messages, phone messages, and more that one receives in a day. Added to that, an average person has about 60,000 thoughts a day – many unfortunately are the same thoughts (and can be self-deprecating).

There is a thorough communication plan in a five-star school. To ensure effective communication is ongoing, you divide all of the staff into *communication cadres* (CCs) of five to six people/teams. Each cadre designates a *communication captain* (which can change monthly). When one person or all in the cadre need to receive a communication (not confidential or private), that person receives the information along with the CC. It is the responsibility of the cadre and captain to ensure everyone has received it, knows their role, and follows through. Not too difficult. It's called TEAMING! YES!

Also, it is important to know the type of communication that is most effective for each individual. The principal and administrative team especially need this valuable information. A simple form can be distributed at the beginning of each year to all staff (or when a new teacher enters the building) that asks for the following:

Name: _____

Date: _____

What is the most effective way to communicate to you (please be specific): email? Face to face? Text message? Hard copy? Phone? Team? Other? _____

_____

All of the above? _____

_____

How do you best process and retain information (your learning style)? _____

_____

What else do I need to know to communicate positively to you? _____

_____

This information is shared with the CC/captain, and it illustrates appreciation of different processing styles. A similar form can be distributed to parents and students at the beginning of the year (a modified version).

To be an effective communicator, you must discover the best way the recipient receives communiqué. Additionally, a five-star school that focuses on effective and positive messages trusts that everyone will:

- Listen more than speak and listen genuinely.

- Be self-aware of body language and tone of voice.

- Work for a win–win outcome, avoiding conflicts, disputes, grievances, and tension.

- Focus on "put ups" rather than "put downs."

- Breathe, calm yourself, and think before you respond.

- Defend the absent – don't allow others to put peers/colleagues down in front of you. Teach this to students.

- Work together to make communication positive, focused, ongoing, and efficient.

- Make ongoing clear, succinct, and extraordinary communication the key to the success of a five-star school.

We know communication is effective when the message is understood, the purpose of the message is realized, the task is completed, and everyone wins. It has been said that a person normally shares positive communications with 3–5 others and negative communications with approximately 11–15 others. Negative statements include:

- That is not my job.

- It is not my fault (blame game).

- That will never work. We tried that in October 1942 – it didn't work then, so it won't work now.

- They get paid the big bucks. Let them figure it out.

- I probably shouldn't tell you this, but . . . . . .

- I know you won't like this idea, but . . . .

- I don't have time.

- I can't worry about how they feel. I am here to teach.

- It is not my problem.

- You are a _____ (name calling) – or he or she is a _____.

- There is not enough time in a day.

> "
> I do not want a new generation of children with high intelligence quotients and low caring quotients; with sharp competitive edges and dull cooperative instincts; with highly developed computer skills, but poorly developed consciences; with gigantic commitment to the big "I" but little sense of responsibility to the bigger "We."
> **Miriam Wright**
> **Edelman Children's**
> **Defense Fund, 2000**
> "

Obviously, you can add many more statements. I would like to address the last one because it is heard so often. The bottom line of reality is – *there will never be more time in a day*. We have 7 days in a week, 24 hours in a day, and 12 months in a year. This is the reality we all need to deal with by developing a plan to make the most of the time we have. It takes work, but it is worth it. Not only do adults need to learn to manage time, we need to teach our students this important skill, starting in elementary school and carrying on through every grade level into college.

In Dale Carnegie's book *How to Win Friends and Influence People,* he provides the subsequent opinion to become an exceptional communicator:

> **"**
> If we were to speak more than we were to listen we would have been given two mouths instead of two ears.
> **(Mark Twain)**
> **"**

- Don't criticize, condemn, or complain.

- Give honest and sincere appreciation.

- Arouse in the other person an eager want.

- Become genuinely interested in other people.

- Remember the person's name and learn to pronounce it correctly (a person's name is the sweetest and most important sound in any language).

- Be an extraordinary listener.

- Encourage others to talk about themselves.

- Talk in terms of other's interests.

- Make others feel important – and do it naturally.

- Have *team time* where team members celebrate the success of their teammates.

- SMILE.

Simply stated, positive communication is caring about others and building relationships. It is the choice of words, body language, listening habits, processing skills, and sincerity. Adults need to ask each other and the students:

1. What are we doing right concerning communication (teaching the skills of speaking, listening, reading, and writing to students)?

2. How can we improve?

3. What will we all *commit* to concerning continuing affirmative communication to F.E.E.D. students?

Once a plan is developed with everyone's input, it is shared. Every person commits to the plan and successful communication becomes a way of life at a five-star school. When communication is recognized and practiced at the staff level, it becomes winning at the student and parent level.

Top-chef teachers realize communication is essential for effective student learning. The best teachers learn how students communicate and how they like to receive communication. They ask who, what, when, where questions and try to avoid questions that just need a yes or no response. And, most importantly, they learn the effectiveness of the *pause.* Some teachers

> It is not happy people who are thankful, it is thankful people who are happy.
> **Source unknown**

have the tendency to go so fast there is never a pause in the lesson or questioning. The quote, "It is the silence between the notes that makes the music," applies to the pause, or silence allowing students to think.

The pause will F.E.E.D. the students and give them they necessary time to process information and to formulate a message to communicate. It also provides structure and gives the teacher time to assess the class; who's listening, on task, wanting to respond, etc. It takes patience and fortitude to produce and recognize the *pause* technique.

To truly F.E.E.D. students, communication is critical. It's not WHAT we say – it's HOW we say it. We know that 7% of communication comes from words, 38% is from the tone of voice, and 55% is our body language. Our new means of communicating mainly via text has done a disservice to our students. They spend so much time texting and through other means that meaningful conversations rarely take place.

Communication involves speaking, listening, reading, writing, behavior, problem-solving, and thinking. Communication must be frequent, timely, accurate, positive (as much as possible), and current. Effective communication solves problems, involves everyone, works toward goals, focuses on respect, shares knowledge, and breeds success.

Speaking

The research is abundant. The main points about communication are that first communication is NOT just speaking. However, to F.E.E.D. students, we must teach them how to become great speakers, avoiding the distractors we hear so often (ah, oh, um, like, and, er, you know what I mean, etc.). Top-chef teachers take pride in modeling valuable speaking techniques through concise, honest, and articulate speech. I was amazed at my 7th–11th grade students this summer on how expressive and remarkable they were when giving oral presentations. Someone is doing an outstanding job in their district teaching students how to speak.

> No printed word nor spoken plea,
> Can teach young minds what they should be.
> Not all the books on all the shelves,
> But what the teachers are themselves
> **author unknown**

Oral communication/speaking is the process by which people send and receive information verbally. Oral communication creates meaning through speech. When students are taught how to be outstanding speakers, they become more confident and productive.

Listening

One of the critical components of communication is listening, which is also one of the least-taught skills in many classrooms. We do not take enough time, or none at all, to teach students how to be effective listeners. What people intend and what others hear

>
> Talk is the most powerful tool of communication in the classroom, and it's fundamentally central to the acts of teaching and learning.
> **Dr. Frank Hardman**
>

are often two different concepts because listeners respond to more than just words. We also observe the tone of voice and the body language. Great listeners respect the speaker and truly listen without interrupting or glazing over. Active listeners are considerate of what is being said, closely listen, and model this for the students. They concentrate on what the speaker is saying, give full attention, and do not let their mind roam. Students need to learn to listen successfully, which includes the stages of the process:

- Hearing and preparing

- Focusing on the message

- Using "I" statements rather than "YOU"

- Grasping and deciphering

- Opening your mind to process what is received

- Using the person's name if appropriate

- Judging the content

- Analyzing and appraising

- Remembering and repeating for clarification

When teaching students how to listen actively, they need to learn to let the speaker know that what was said was heard both accurately and enthusiastically.

Equipping students with effective communication skills results in higher levels of emotional intelligence, higher test scores, lowering occurrences of bullying, and advancements in complete mental well-being. There is so much to achieve from applying these skills.

Active listeners encourage rich discussions and demonstrate responsiveness. Sound listening reflects courtesy and positive etiquettes. F.E.E.D. students by helping them become extraordinary communicators. Teach students to use the EAR model:

E: EXPLORE. Use open-ended questions and observe non-
    verbal messages.

> **"**
> The most important thing in communication is hearing what isn't said.
> **Dr. Peter Drucker**
> **""**

A: ACKNOWLEGE. Acknowledge by para-phrasing what you believe was said.

R: RESPOND. Respond using the least amount of time.

Reading and Writing

TOP CHEF TEACHERS know the importance of reading and writing for students and continuously stress this to the students. When deficiencies are identified, we must do whatever possible to try and bring students up to grade level. The further they get, the more difficult it becomes. That is why I am such a big fan of journaling; students write on a topic and then share it with the class.

As discussed in Chapter 4, research shows we absorb 10% of what we read, 20% of what is heard, 30% by looking at pictures, 50% by seeing and hearing, such as watching a movie, 70% by participating in a discussion, and 90% by presenting and/or simulating real-life experiences. Even as a math teacher, I always stress the importance of reading and writing efficiently to become victorious. We need to realize that the new workplace demands exceptional communication abilities.

F.O.O.D (Fulfilling Opportunities Offered Daily) for Thought

Review suggestions for enhancing communication as a staff and to students:

✓ Have the *staff* determine all the ways we communicate (i.e., crying, eye contact, words, sounds, silence etc.) and give real-life examples of students. Role play successful and ineffectual ways to communicate.

✓ List strategies used to teach students successful communica-tion methods.

✓ Discuss students who struggle with communicating successfully and list characteristics. Include strategies to assist these students.

✓ Identify a collaborative environment and how we can increase com-munication opportunities within daily routines and activities.

✓ Have teachers view a recent video of a lesson being taught. Deter-mine the amount of time for reflection, questioning, active listening, and hopefully journaling. Do a self-assessment of your lesson, stu-dent responses, and involvement.

✓ Develop a TO BE list rather than a TO DO list: I want TO BE: happy, successful, caring, loved, etc. Have the students write their own TO BE list during the first week of school and throughout the year.

✓ Have teams discuss ways to teach listening to students and effectively model active listening.

✓ Have the staff/teams review the schoolwide communication plan and determine if there are gaps or areas needing to be improved.

✓ Get each staff member the book *Teaching Kids to Thrive; Essential Skills for Success* by Debbie Silver and Dedra Stafford, and have a discussion about what strategies and activities you will try with your students. Everyone reports back at another staff meeting to assess what was done and how students responded.

10 Team-Building Games for the First Day of Class

Team-building activities are great. Not only can they help establish routines, tone, and expectations, they're also fun, and can help learners feel comfortable. Though many older students in high school and college may groan at their thought, they're usually fun and great ways to help students feel at ease. Before you dismiss them as too juvenile, try one. You might be surprised.

Note that which game you choose, your rules for the game, and any revisions to the rules depend on the nature of the class you're using them with. Certain students may feel overly liberated – especially in middle school – with the idea of a "game," and so expectations must be carefully given to younger K–8 learners – and even 9–12 – to ensure that every student is set up for success.

1. Me Too!

Ideal Grade Levels: K–20

First student gives a fact about themselves – I love basketball, I have two sisters, etc. If that statement or fact is true about another student, they stand up and say "Me too!" They can also stay seated, but simply raise their hand and say "Me too!"

(Continued)

2. Park Bench

Ideal Grade Levels: 6–20

Two chairs are placed together to resemble a park bench. Two students volunteer – or are selected – to act out "what happened" in a fictional news story. They are given 1 minute to prepare a scene where they discuss the "event" without every actually saying what happened. After a given time period (1–5 minutes), peers guess "what happened," but they must give up all four important details: Who, What, Where, and When. For example:

> What: College basketball game
> Who: Kentucky and Kansas
> When: Early April
> Where: New Orleans

3. Fact or Fiction

Ideal Grade Levels: 3–12

In a circle, first a student offers two facts and one piece of fiction about themselves. Others raise their hand or are called on to identify which were facts and which were fiction. The correct guesser goes next. Play is completed when all students have gone.

4. Green Door

Ideal Grade Levels: 5–20

Leader chooses a topic, but keeps it quiet, only saying that "You can bring a ____ through the green door." Students are then forced to deduce the topic by asking if other things can be brought through the green door as well, e.g., "Can I bring a ____ through the green door?"

Leader can only reply yes or no. When topic is identified, topic resets. Topics can be content related, such as parts of speech, colors, geometric figures, historical figures, etc.

5. One-Minute Talk

Ideal Grade Levels: 5–20

Students are chosen to give 60-second talks on anything, from self-selected topics they are passionate about, have specific expertise in, etc., to topics given from the teacher.

6. Count to Ten

Ideal Grade Levels: 3–20

All students stand in a circle. First student says "1," or "1, 2." The next student picks up where that student left off and can say a maximum number of 2 numbers. The movement continues clockwise until it gets to 10, where that student has to sit, and the game starts back over at 1 at the next student. Note that there can be no pausing or silent counting – any pauses or indications the student is counting/calculating forces them to sit. Also, pouting or talking during counting results in elimination from future rounds. The big idea is to count strategically so that you can keep from saying "10."

7. I Never

Ideal Grade Levels: K–20

Students form a circle. First student says something they've never done. Each student that *has* done the thing the other student has not steps briefly into the center. The game continues until every person has stated something they've done.

8. Magic Ball

Ideal Grade Levels: K–20

Students form a circle. First student is "given" an imaginary magic ball. Student sculpts the imaginary ball into a new shape, handing it to the person to their right. Activity is silent. Any talking/noise results in student sitting. After game, guessing may be done to predict what the "sculpture" was.

9. Line

Ideal Grade Levels: K–8

Students are given a criteria and must silently put themselves in a line as quickly as possible, to meet a goal, compete against other classes, or receive some reward (free reading time, no homework, etc.). The criteria can be simple (birthdays), or slightly more complicated (alphabetical order of college or career ambition).

10. Inside-Outside Circle

Ideal Grade Levels: 3–20

Students form a circle within a circle with (ideally) an equal number of students in both circles. Inside circle members pair

(Continued)

with outside circle members. Activity leader (usually teacher, but can be a student) presents a topic, prompt, or question. Partners share for 10 seconds (or less), leader asks inside circle to move clockwise a certain number of spaces to collaborate with new partners directly across from them. This is usually content focused, and helps spur quick discussion on content-related topics, or even current events.

Source: The Advisory Book by Linda Crawford

Via TeachThought.

This article appeared on TeachThought on August 8, 2012, and was written by the TeachThought team.

The communication focus being set and strong, we now move on to an important aspect of education—being F.E.D and dealing with all of the stressors of life and school.

EIGHT ACTIONS

MY BEST TEACHERS DID TO F.E.E.D. ME

1. Encourged me.

2. Took time to understand me.

3. Gave me resources to better myself.

4. Always showed their appreciation.

5. Lifted me up.

6. Whenever I was down, they'd cheer me up.

7. Gave me wisdom.

8. They all made sure we were confident in our own skin.

To | Mrs. Storr, Ms. Walker, and Ms. Jones
by | Alana McCord, 9th grader

Who's to Blame?

The college professor said:
"Such rawness in a student is a shame, lack of preparation in high school is to blame."

Said the high school teacher:
"Good heavens! That boy's a fool. The fault of course is with the middle school."

The middle school teacher said:
"From stupidity may I be spared. They sent him in so unprepared."

The primary teacher huffed:
"Kindergarten blockheads all. They call that preparation – why, it's worse than none at all."

The kindergarten teacher said:
"Such lack of training never did I see. What kind of woman must that mother be."

The mother said:
"Poor helpless child. He's not to blame. His father's people were all the same."

Said the father at the end of the line:
"I doubt the rascal's even mine."

Anonymous

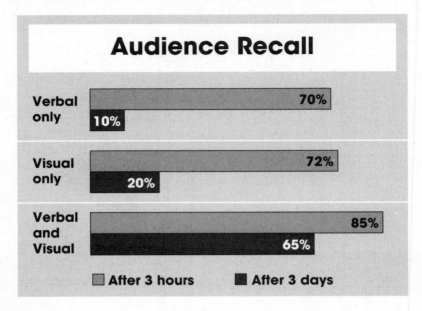

Audience Recall

	After 3 hours	After 3 days
Verbal only	70%	10%
Visual only	72%	20%
Verbal and Visual	85%	65%

> *Because of the rapid changes both technological and social, it is becoming less possible to operate our lives effectively using old paradigms. The learners today will be living in a society that will require its citizens to think constructively, make sound decisions, solve problems, access information and take responsibility for their own lives. The educational challenge is to build essential skills for learners in preparation for adult life.*
>
> **Source unknown**

> *Young people are empowered to the extent that they are seen by others as resources, make contributions to society, and feel free of threats to their safety.*
>
> **author unknown**

Percent	Children with High Self-Esteem
80%	Kids entering 1st grade
20%	Kids entering 5th grade
5%	Kids entering high school

40 OLD-FASHIONED SKILLS THAT KIDS NEED TO KNOW TODAY!

- How to write a letter
- How to make a phone call
- How to take a message
- How to get to know an older person
- How to play with a baby
- How to sew on a button
- How to make a genuine apology
- How to read slowly
- How to hammer a nail
- How to shake hands
- How to introduce yourself
- How to take notice of needs around you
- How to make scrambled eggs
- How to balance a checkbook
- How to see a job through to completion
- How to write a thank-you note
- How to do laundry
- How to take care of a garden
- How to fix something instead of replace it
- How to plan a healthy meal
- How to hang a picture
- How to wash dishes

- How to make a budget
- How to wait and save for something
- How to check tire pressure
- How to ask questions to get to know someone better
- How to read a map
- How to find a book in the library
- How to seek counsel from someone more experienced
- How to care for a pet
- How to select a gift that the receiver will appreciate
- How to admit a mistake
- How to set the table
- How to iron a shirt
- How to give someone the benefit of the doubt
- How to weigh out the pro's and con's of a decision
- How to have good table manners
- How to read a recipe
- How to attend a concert or performance
- How to do something well, even if no one is watching
- How to be KIND!

https://frugalfun4boys.com

CHAPTER 8

Satisfaction: We Left F.E.D. and Eager to Return

A Focus on Attitude and Dealing with Stress

The goal of a five-star restaurant is to ensure that every guest leaves Fulfilled, Energized, and De-stressed (F.E.D.). The team wants people to feel and go to any length to make it happen. As indicated, upon entering you are greeted by a host that makes you feel valued and significant and the second you arrive at the table someone is there to bring you water, possibly a tray of goodies and begin the experience. A sense of calm overcomes the diners. When you first arrive at this elegant restaurant you are usually professionally showered by servers making sure your immediate needs are met. You feel cherished and appreciated.

In a FIVE STAR SCHOOL, the mission is for *everyone* to leave at the end of the day also feeling F.E.D. (Fueled, Energized, De-stressed). This is difficult, especially for teachers with everything they go through in a given day. Many times their goal is to get home and take a nap (ah – yes!). As I drive home after a long day with many interactions and surprises, I really try to focus on the great things that happened that day, what/who made me laugh (you will always find something to laugh about, no matter what grade level, and if you don't, find another profession), and whether there is something I would have done or handled differently. I attempt to keep my thoughts positive, realizing that you should never worry about something *you can't control*. I can't change the sequence of the day or how I engaged or interacted with students, and yes, we all do make mistakes and have regrets. As long as I get up the next day and am excited about going back, life is great. I want to leave F.E.D.

Fulfilled

A top-chef teacher realizes that teaching is a fulfilling job. They make a difference for students every day. It is challenging, of course, because students look to you for advice, personal support, positive connections, and as a role model. There is a lot of pressure on teachers. The best features of being a teacher are seeing a student "click" that they finally got it, working with remarkable colleagues, never being bored, watching students flourish, and laughing every day.

Fulfillment comes from one entity – your *attitude*. I truly believe that your attitude can make or break your day, and sometimes we have to take a personal moment to step away from the classroom/situation and have an attitude adjustment. Your attitude determines your success. Attitude is your foundation and success is your kitchen where you make all of the magic transpire.

John C. Maxwell writes that to be successful with a great attitude "we all need to work to be the MVP and can be if we are VALUABLE:

V – Visualizes what can be, not just what is.

A – Appreciates the other players.

L – Leads by example.

U – Understands the BIG picture.

A – Adds value to the entire room.

B – Brings home the bacon.

L – Learns quickly from mistakes.

E – Encourages others."

Attitude

Attitude is a habitual mode of thoughts and feelings. A Harvard study showed that when a person gets a job or promotion, 85% of the time it is because of attitude and 15% due to intelligence and knowledge of specific details and facts. Attitudes are the state of mind and dispositions that affect behavior and change regularly. A positive attitude means that the top team of chefs work together in helping one another out and focusing on what is working and differences they make. When we take care of each other, the students are going to be rewarded in the long run.

> Yesterday is history, tomorrow is a mystery, and today is a gift. That's why it's called the PRESENT.
> **Source unknown**

Our *attitude of gratitude* lets others know that we first expect the best from ourselves and then from others. I can remember my mother always asking me after a test or a basketball/softball game – "Did you do your best?" Most times I would say yes. However, for those times where I said no, we would then scrutinize my response. That is one question I continually ask my students – did you *try* and did you do *your best?* My mother used to also say "Wake up, get up, dress up, show up, be up, and never give up." She was a wise woman.

Your attitude is far more crucial than your aptitude. Professionals say that people who have a positive attitude are happier, healthier, and more productive than those with a negative point of view. When I wake up in the morning (by Alexa playing my favorite music), I respond to the fact that I am awake and above ground (which is great) and then I have a morning ritual that ends with, "This is going to be a FABULOUS day." I want to start my day on a positive note. Now, do I ever have a bad day? Of course, everyone does, but I try to steer clear of negatives at all costs. Attitude is the foundation; success is the structure.

A teacher I met many years ago, Jack M. Argenio from Woodrow Wilson Middle School, Connecticut, shared his story:

> **❝**
> I walk into the classroom and write P-A-C-E on the board. I look closely at every student in the room—directly into each of their eyes. I then ask if anyone knows what P-A-C-E stands for? After many guesses, I explain that it means Positive Attitudes Change Everything. We begin a great discussion of what that implies. I then give each student a piece of paper and ask them to write a short paragraph on "Why I Think I'm Special." They can sign their names or not. I collect the papers and read them to the class minus the names. I then explain that every one of them is unique and exceptional. I discuss attitude, accountability and responsibility—they are responsible for everything they say and do in school, the classroom, and the world. I discuss assessment and finish with the fact that the only students who will fail in my class are those who fail to try.
> **❞**

A focus on a positive attitude and a wonderful lesson that teams can do with students.

A positive attitude for adults and students is important for increasing teamwork and inspiring others. It breeds loyalty, solves problems, improves quality, and reduces stress. Some notes I took at a conference (presenter unknown) gave steps to create and sustain a positive attitude:

- Make a habit of getting it done and not procrastinating.
- Have an attitude of gratitude.
- Learn how to teach students to be positive.
- Change the scene and find the positive in each circumstance.
- Don't sweat the small stuff.

- Write in your journal what you are thankful for and reread this on a bad day.

- Avoid negative influences and conversations (watch out for the D.U.C.K.S.).

- Start every day with a positive thought or action.

Success and failure in schools and life is influenced by your attitude. It is a habit and a way of doing and responding to daily occurrences. It is difficult to change another's attitude but with a lot of constant effort it can possibly be done ultimately. It is very difficult to work *for* or with a "lemon sandwich eater" – someone who is always complaining and whining. They try to take your day but you can't let them have it. In these cases, you can attempt to address the negativity (which sometimes works) or completely steer clear of the person.

We need to teach students that to be winning, you must think, act, talk, and behave like a successful person. And that they can often adjust their lives just by changing their attitude. The mind is such a powerful instrument, and just by focusing on thoughts and feelings we can begin to see the same situation differently. I try to have my students work through situations by asking them, "How would they have handled that differently?" The responses vary, but give them all some thought-provoking "a-ha's." Attitudes are learned and not the same as behavior. We may think one way but act another, or change our thinking because of behavior. Our goal is to align the two positively.

My father always said, "Don't get into a discussion with anyone about religion or politics (especially today)" because it will not be a win–win situation. I wish we could have more positive conversations about controversial topics, because that is when I learn. We know our experiences, influence of others, and exposure to life affect our attitude. We must realize that also when dealing with our students. Where do they come from, what are their learnings, and how are they influenced are three great areas for top-chef teams to discuss. I know that some of my students have seen and done things that I have no connection to or could imagine.

> **"**
> There are wooden ships, there are sailing ships, there are ships that sail to sea, but the best ships are friendships, and may they always be.
>
> **Irish proverb**
> **"**

We want to teach students to learn to have an attitude of integrity, care, and compassion and model this as educators. When I see students helping others, I get excited. We carry into our adulthood many attitudes established as students in our younger years; that is why the role of top-chef teachers is so important. Success or failure for students correlates with both teacher and student attitudes.

Energized

You know the minute your feet hit the floor in the morning if you have energy or not. You can tell on your ride to work and you can tell which colleagues are energized. At our school we are blessed to have Katie McCloud, who is our language arts curriculum coordinator and PD leader. To me, Katie embodies "energized." You always see her zipping around the school, busily multitasking with a big smile on her face making others' days. I always look forward to seeing Katie because she energizes me.

Energized means ready to attack the day with gusto and excitement. The top-chef teacher is excited about teaching and displays great physical and emotional health. Health is important to top-chef teachers because everyone knows that when you feel good about yourself, you walk it and talk it. Energized means you like being you and have a positive self-concept/esteem.

The self-concept is what top-chef teachers believe about themselves and their own personal attributes and values. These beliefs affect motives, actions, behavior, and skills. The self-concept involves how you feel about self, think about self, and demonstrate a self-confidence that suggests you have a positive attitude and feel fulfilled. I believe a person with a secure self-concept is generally happy and is an extraordinary role model for helping students build their self-esteem.

To assist students in enhancing their self-esteem (feelings about self) we must first model it. Show our students that we like who we are and we can F.E.E.D. them frequently. We then build a climate for success teaching skills and focusing on strengths rather than limitations. We recognize, respect, and encourage each student, providing a safe environment where students can ask questions, take risks, and share concerns. And of course we *smile* and know their name, looking forward to something special they can bring to each day.

We want our students to feel great, look great, and be great. A positive self-concept and self-esteem links to beliefs that you can be successful while others look to you as blossoming. A flourishing student energizes us and lets top-chef teachers know they truly are making a difference. Again, our energizing positive self-concept continues to influence opinions, emotions, and conduct. Having a positive self-esteem is part of emotional intelligence. With a positive self-concept/esteem we can deal with stress.

De-Stressed

There is only one group of people who do not have any stress in their lives; those who are no longer with us. Stress is a common factor in teaching; especially today where teachers are also needed to be mom, dad, nurse, counselor, coach, and wear a multitude of hats. Stress affects everyone is

> **"**
> If you always do what you've
> always done, you'll always
> get what you've always
> gotten (definition of insanity).
> **Source unknown**
> **"**

different ways. The top-chef teachers on teams learn to recognize stress, analyze it, deal with it, and learn from it.

What is stress? It is the normal response to proceedings that make you feel exposed or intimidated, or upsets the balance in your life. We all need balance in our lives. Another definition that I found is "the confusion created when one's mind supersedes the body's desire to choke the living daylights out of some jerk who desperately needs it" (source unknown). And we all have felt that way. Stress is a natural and manageable part of life. It is the way in which we react physically, mentally, and/or emotionally to innumerable circumstances, changes, and demands of life. The stress we undergo is engrained in the "fight or flight" reaction, during which our bodies experience physical changes that prepare us to respond to an exciting or threatening state of affairs. Once the condition has passed or is under control, our stress response diminishes, permitting us to relax. However, the constant demands of academic or personal life can prevent us from becoming fully peaceful and can lead to stress overload. Stress that is constant or builds up over time and is not controlled efficiently can have serious outcomes to your health and overall quality of life.

Certain beliefs can cause stress if you permit it:

➤ Work/life is a struggle; it need not be if you are prepared, excited, and love *you.*

➤ The end product is more important than the experience; it's the journey that counts, not the destination.

➤ Doing and having are more important that being; we are HUMAN BEINGS not HUMAN DOINGS.

➤ There is not enough time to get everything done; make time!

➤ Quantity is more important than quality; I want quality of life rather than quantity of years.

➤ People; you must have encouraging and passionate people skills to be in this profession.

Educators are stressed today. I just read where a small college was closing its education department because of the lack of students. I truly was astounded. We have spoken of teacher shortages for years but it may soon become a reality. Teachers must prepare so many different meals for so many different students and their learning styles that it is overwhelming.

To deal with stress, we must manage our:

- ✓ *Emotions.* What makes you tense or anxious? What do you need to do?

- ✓ *Time.* How do you manage time? What does your day or week look like? Do you build time in for you? Your family? Your friends?

- ✓ *Energies.* Where do you spend most of your energy? How do you get energized? What do you need to do today to start focusing on you?

- ✓ *Professional life.* Do you love what you do? Do you maximize the day when at work and let go when at home? What are your assets and needs?

- ✓ *Personal life.* How is your life? What would you do differently? Are YOU #1 in your life? If not, who is?

Two of the major mechanisms of your stress level, as told to me recently, is how much water we drink and the foods we consume. These directly affect stress. Also, the relationships between administrators and colleagues make a major difference. I ascertained many years ago that "people don't quit jobs—they quit *bosses.*" I personally can relate to that statement. We don't have to *love* the people we work with, but it is beneficial to at least respect our teammates/colleagues and look forward to the workday.

Students are also stressed. Do we have programs and people in place to help students with their stress? There are many issues that cause our students stress today. It can be from home situations, bullying, lack of skills, different viewpoints and backgrounds, race, ethnicity, religion, sexual orientation, weight, and many other areas. These need to be addressed. I had students come to me last year and privately discuss that they were gay and were being bullied. I felt grateful that they felt secure coming to me but felt sad that we had no programs in place to openly discuss this issue. So we just began our own group that would get together when needed to share.

These are the AAAs of stress management: *Alter* how you can remove stress; attempt to *Avoid* the source of the stress, and *Accept* how to live with the stress (source unknown).

Dr. Debbie Silver, a wonderful presenter and friend, identifies 11 factors you can execute to lessen stress in your life:

1. Make someone's day brighter each day – students, staff, colleagues, parents, administrative team, and/or the principal.

2. Keep only cheerful friends. Grouches pull you down – avoid them.

3. Keep learning whatever interests you.

4. Enjoy the simple things.

5. Let the tears happen. Endure, grieve, and move on. The only person who is with us our entire life is ourself. Be alive while alive. Life is not a spectator sport.

6. Surround yourself with what your love. Your classroom can be your refuge.

7. Cherish your health. If it is great – preserve it. If it is unstable, improve it, and if it is beyond help – GET HELP.

8. Don't take guilt trips. Go visit another class or school. Take time out, travel, read, spend time with family and friends. Do not trek to guilt land.

9. Tell the people you love that you love them at every opportunity. Remember, the most unlovable are those who need our love the most.

10. Laugh often, long, and loud. Laugh until you can't breathe. Laugh so much that you can be pursued in school by your distinctive laughter.

11. And, learn to deal with *change*. In our profession, change is ongoing, frustrating, and aggravating, but many times is needed and improves our surroundings.

Change

Change is the only constant in our society and occurs on a daily basis in education. We have heard "shift happens." It is a fact of life, inevitable, and occurs regularly as reflected in weather, our moods, the seasons, and football rankings. Without change we stagnate, lack innovation, and become set in our ways. Change involves new ways to achieve success and become aware of our personal and professional purpose. The change process can bring out the best and worst in people.

When first introduced, change can be difficult for up to 95% of the population. Most people resist change while a small percent thrive on it. Since we are creatures of habit, we adhere to what is routine to us. We unconsciously organize our frame of reference out of all experiences that we internalize and believe to be true. Since we espouse our personal judgment as authentic, our frame of reference becomes part of our personality. Change disrupts and disorients this frame of reference. It can cause fear, anger, or increased anxiety.

We try to convince ourselves that we are up-to-date and modern, yet we are a lot more traditional. We welcome innovations that make our life more convenient and label them "progress." Nevertheless, we don't have the same

kind of enthusiasm for the types of change
that affect our professions. Many oppose
change at the workplace because of a threat
to their security. Even when we agree that
the old way is not working, any attempt to
alter a comfortable working arrangement causes anxiety.

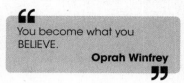

**You become what you
BELIEVE.**
                Oprah Winfrey

In my educational experiences, I have seen reasons change is not easy.
My analysis has concluded:

- ✓ *Two out of every three teachers suffer from low or lack of self-esteem.*
  (J. Canfield). I agree with Canfield – there are educators who do
  not feel good about themselves. When they are trying to deal with
  their lack of internal confidence, it is very difficult to even contem-
  plate any change to their external environment.

- ✓ *Many are in a R.U.T. (Repeating Unproductive Tasks).* We are creatures
  of habit. However, many times the habits we nurture do not produce the results desired. Recall the definition of insanity.

- ✓ *You can't do something you don't know how to do.* Some people are just
  not able to change because the just don't have the skills to cope with
  change. If a person is already having difficulty teaching, change is
  even more intimidating.

- ✓ *Overloading will negatively impact any change.* We are so guilty of overloading in education. We get excited about one program and begin
  implementation, then another program comes along and we add it
  on. Unfortunately, asking for too many changes all at once usually
  results in a lack of quality. For lasting and positive results, it is prac-
  tical to implement one major change at a time.

- ✓ *There are a lot of "war stories" of "we've done this before.* It didn't work
  then and it won't work now." People with battle scars of previous
  change ventures – especially unsuccessful ones – are more prone to
  openly oppose any change. There are individuals who hold meetings
  for the D.U.C.K.S to gather and criticize the efforts of the one who
  brought about the change.

- ✓ *Negaholics.* Every school has at least a few D.U.C.K.S. (Dependent
  Upon Criticizing and Killing Success) who thrive on complaining
  and they quack their day away having frequent *quack attacks.* The
  D.U.C.K.S. turn teachers' lounges into duck ponds.

Change is not easy. It takes time, commitment, patience, and a belief in
improvement. Everyone involved must focus on strengths, move slowly,
and work together. Accept the challenge of change. We must work collaboratively by encouraging one another to shine and strive for excellence.
We must stop blaming and complaining and begin daring and caring to

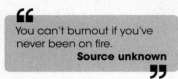

F.E.E.D. students. Just remember the great song by Bob Dylan, "The Times They Are a-Changing," and ask yourself if you can change with the times.

Please recall that your life is meant to be enjoyed *now*. Not on the weekend, break, summer, vacation, or after retirement, but *now*. Seize the day and look at each day as a gift that you unwrap slowly, carefully, and with patience. Remember, "to the world you are one person, but to one person you may be their world" (source unknown).

F.O.O.D (Fulfilling Opportunities Offered Daily) for Thought

The following are specific activities that you can do to become satisfied with your life and job:

- Ask teams to do an attitude analysis and see if they need an attitude adjustment or to share their self-realization.

- Develop a set of questions that the team can ask students about doing their best and trying.

- Discuss self-esteem with your teammates and identify what you do to help one another and students develop a positive self-worth.

- List all of the indicators of a stressed-out teacher and student. Discuss and share where you are individually. Discuss student stress and how we teach them how to deal with it. Look at all the areas and determine if there are outlets in the school for students to be heard (bullying, race, sexual orientation, religion, home situations, weight, suicide, and other areas that relate to your population).

- Have the staff write letters to each other outlining the extraordinary qualities you demonstrate on a daily basis. Have students also write letters to their teachers.

- Take time to discuss time management, how it affects lives, what you can do, and managing your priorities.

- Work with students in defining what a great attitude looks like and what they need to be doing. Develop a personal attitude plan with goals and steps for success.

- Have students define "success" and role play what a successful person looks like, does, says, and acts.

- Realize that students learn to handle stress from parents/adults in their lives and need to be given mechanisms to deal. Discuss this as a team/staff and list strategies.

- Share "Life's Seven Cardinal Rules" prior to a staff meeting and discuss what stands out, makes you think, or is something one needs to adopt:

> "
> There are two gifts we should give our children:
> one is roots, the other is wings.
> **Holding Carter Jr.**
> "

   1. *Make peace with your past so it doesn't spoil your present.* Your past does not define your future – your *actions, attitude,* and *beliefs* do!
   2. *What others think of you does not really matter.* It's how much you value yourself that is important!
   3. *Time heals almost everything* – give TIME . . . TIME.
   4. *No one is in charge of your happiness except yourself.* Waste no time and effort searching for peace and joy in the world outside. Look inside. You are in control of your "happiness backpack" (another great activity is to have staff and/or students give a presentation of what is in their happiness backpack – what makes them happy).
   5. *Don't compare your life to others.* You have no idea what their journey is all about. If we all threw our problems in a pile and saw everyone else's, we would grab our own back as quickly as possible.
   6. *Stop thinking too much.* It's all right not to know all of the answers. Sometimes there is no answer, not going to be any answer, never has been an answer. That's the answer – accept it and move on. NEXT?
   7. *SMILE.* You don't own all of the problems in the world. A smile can brighten the darkest day and make someone's life beautiful. It is a curve to turn a life around and set everything straight. And remember. . . . "Don't drop your smile!" (I say, "You dropped your smile" and point to the floor when I see a grouchy student walking through the hallway. Inevitably, the student looks down and then many even look up at me and smile. I also do this in airports, banks, and stores. Love the reactions I get.)

- Ask students to discuss the topics self-concept and self-esteem, define them, and identify where their self-esteem falls on a scale of 1–10. Opens up a significant discussion.

- Ask students to share their stressors in life, school, and with peers. Develop a schoolwide plan to deal with the issue of stress and trauma in students' lives (which is growing in our society).

- Find effective videos and presentations on YouTube on students' stress and discuss as a faculty.

- Share the following https://www.7cups.com/exercises/mindfulness1 with the staff so they can learn to relax and meditate. Depending on the age level of students, you can share with them.

Once we are F.E.D., we can look at the importance of feedback and how to make it useful.

CHAPTER 9

Comment Card: The Opportunity to Provide Feedback

Honest Feedback Is Crucial to F.E.E.D. Students and Equip Their Future

At a five-star restaurant you are constantly asked how everything is, if you need anything, and how we can help you. You are given the opportunity to provide feedback to the staff. Honest feedback is essential. And the best restaurants take it to heart and learn from authentic feedback with the customer's always right philosophy. The two words you will hear after feedback is "MY PLEASURE." A five-star restaurant takes feedback as crucial and learns from any negative feedback by making changes and satisfying customers.

In a five-star school, learning is based on the skills of learning how to learn, relevance, differentiation of curriculum, diversity, a failure-is-not-fatal belief system, and feedback. Five-star schools know that honest feedback is crucial for preparing students for their future.

In my opinion, the ambitions of an effective school are to encourage students to:

- Appreciate education and develop a joy for learning.
- Respect who they are – physically, intellectually, socially, and emotionally.
- Realize they are responsible for their own behavior and must deal with the consequences.
- Learn how to learn.
- Acquire a strong work ethic.
- Appreciate the importance of trying and succeeding – with failure sometimes in between.
- Develop a sense of honesty and integrity.
- Understand how to respect diversity, differences, and determination.
- Strive to set and accomplish goals.
- Learn to receive and give valuable and authentic feedback.

131

> **I hear and I forget.**
> **I see and I believe.**
> **I do and I understand.**
> **Confucius**

Feedback is so important to F.E.E.D. the students so they don't S.T.A.R.V.E. because it empowers students to diagnose their achievements and continue to grow as well as understanding where they need to advance and transform. Feedback is essentially information about the performance or behavior to be affirmed or improved. And with feedback, timing is significant. As addressed previously, students prefer immediate feedback so it can set the groundwork for what comes next. Obviously, feedback needs to be given in the most positive way possible.

Students who struggle with classwork feel frustrated. It is critical that teachers show the students exactly where they went wrong and how one can improve. Showing them ways to do better may also contribute to motivating them.

According to Jane Burgneay (April 2013), someone getting feedback can respond in any of several ways:

- Anger – "I've had enough of this."

- Denial – "I can't see any problem with that."

- Blame – "it's not my fault." (What can you expect when the patient won't listen?)

- Rationalize – "I've had a bad week. Doesn't everyone do this?"

- Acceptance – "I see now."

- Renewed action – "Let me rethink, restart, recreate, and redo."

We need to then teach our students how to receive and give feedback and determine what needs to be done to make necessary changes. Feedback is a fundamental ingredient in the assessment development and must be constructive, not destructive. It also gives us an indication of our performance and effectiveness in providing and receiving communication. Feedback is also a skill that must be taught and processed by students and staff.

Feedback allows teachers to assess students to determine how quickly and correctly they are learning the skill being taught. Ongoing feedback forces the teacher to identify the key learning points and individual students' knowledge base. Valuable feedback enlightens, reinforces, and motivates while delineating the learning expectations. Feedback is a productive way to foster and enrich learning and fundamental aptitudes for understanding.

Skills for Learning

I have been in education for a very long time and love the profession. I am confused, however, that in this day and age testing takes priority over all other rudiments of the true art and science of teaching. Being in the classroom, I have noticed on a daily basis one consistency: the lack of skills by many of my students. I believe the most important Techniques Improving the Performance of Staff and Students (T.I.P.S.) for students is to teach them abilities and how useful skill development is in achieving success. Some staff also need a review of skills and how to incorporate them into daily instruction and life.

Esther Care, Alvin Vista, and Helyn Kim, in association with the Global Economy and Development, Center for Universal Education, have written several articles on the changing education landscape. They note that crucial skills such as communication, problem-solving, and critical thinking are being recognized not just in the United States but all over the world. The real world requires proficiencies to be effective. Additionally, essential skills include but are not limited to learning how to learn through:

- *Reading and writing.* Students are taught these skills from the first time they enter school and hopefully they are reinforced at home.

- *Speaking and listening.* Two of the most neglected skills that are not formerly taught. Students must learn how to be great listeners and excellent speakers without using distractors like "um," "and," "like," "you know what I mean" and to be clear and concise.

- *Studying.* Most students don't study because they have not been taught how to study. Students remember the first 15 minutes of a study period and the last 10–15 minutes. Therefore, they need to be taught to shorten their study time and focus on the most important information. According to Dr. Jill Seibert, "Study skills are fundamental to academic competence."

- *Note-taking.* If student were taught how to take notes before they got to high school, they would be so much better prepared. Note-taking is vital to be successful, and how to use their notes to study and for open-book exams is an additional skill. To F.E.E.D. students we can teach them to use the left side of their paper to list the main ideas being discussed and the right side to identify the facts supporting these ideas. This then becomes a first-rate studying tool.

> **"**
> The purpose of staff development is not just to implement instructional innovations; its central purpose is to build strong collaborative work cultures that will develop the long term capacity for change.
> **Michael Fullan**
> **"**

- *Organizing.* Many of staff and students can use an extensive presentation on how to organize materials, your day, and your life. Students need to be taught to write down their assignments in an agenda book, learn to develop a short "to do" list, and learn to reflect. Time management is an element of organization that also needs to be taught.

- *Researching.* Students must know the steps in conducting research to be successful in high school and ultimately college.

- *Testing.* Few hours are spent on reviewing how to successfully take a test. Since this is the main focus presently of our education system, this is one skill that needs much deliberation.

- *Thinking and problem-solving.* How to think through a problem and become a problem solver is relevant in everyone's personal and school life. This is a skill that is used when dealing with peers, family members, and situations causing anxiety.

- *Decision-making.* Many of our students are unsuccessful because of the decisions they make. Students need to know the process and the consequences that come with their choices.

- *Conflict resolution and how to deal with stress.* In a society with so much bullying in schools, students have to have conflict resolution skills so the outcome is win–win. Stress is also common and must be addressed (Chapter 8)

- *Goal setting.* Teaching students to set goals, work toward them, and achieve them productively is necessary. Goals are dreams with deadlines, so we want our students to learn to turn their dreams into goals.

- *Journaling.* Teach students at a young age how to journal; this can set a habit for life. Through journaling, students learn about themselves and have an outlet to vent, dream, hope, and vision. It is also a form of self-evaluation.

- *Being responsible.* Responsibility is the head of the school also. By giving students jobs, assignments, and opportunities, they learn how to be responsible.

- *Being respectful.* To earn respect, one must give respect. However, there are students that truly do not know what respect looks like. It is crucial to teach.

> Enthusiasm is the match that lights the candle of achievement.
> **William Arthur Ward**

- *Visioning and thinking about the future.* Discuss visioning with students and allow them to think about their future and what it will look like.

- *Feedback.* Explain to the teacher what parts of the lesson are understood, confusing, causing anxiety, and unable to be processed.

Again, there are many articles, books, blogs, and journals covering each of the above in more detail. The purpose of this overview is to bring awareness to the fact that many students do not succeed because they don't have the tools, know what to do, or have mastered the skills. TOP CHEFS conduct a skills analysis with their students to comprehend their level of proficiencies. They teach students the foundation of skills and how to apply them to learning.

David Thornburg wrote about workforce skills in his 2002 book *The New Basics: Education and the Future of Work in the Telematic Age.* He listed the six most desired workforce skills as:

> **"**
> Research says that professional development has to be directly connected to daily work with students, related to content areas, organized around real problems of practice instead of abstractions, continuous and ongoing, and able to provide teachers with access to outside resources and expertise. Professional development should take place within a professional community, a team or network, or both. Changing practice is a difficult and long-term proposition that can't be handled by going off to a workshop. Teachers have to practice change and continually work with others on debugging the problems they encounter.
> **Linda Darling-Hammond**
> **"**

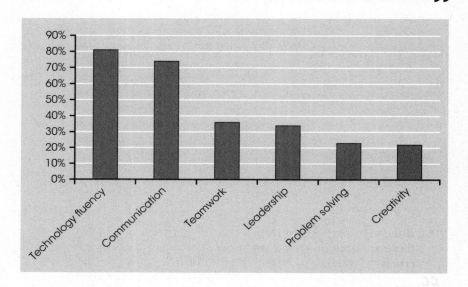

Lynn Karoly and Stan Panis (*The Twenty-First Century at Work,* 2004) "confirm the role of technology in future of work. Considering the rapidly changing nature of technology, the collective conclusion that future workers will have to be learners is also not surprising." To teach all of these skills, educators need specific recipes for each. We then want to effortlessly incorporate each skill into our teachings with concrete illustrations and time to practice.

T.I.P.S.: Techniques Improving the Performance of Staff and Students

Effective professional development empowers educators to *obtain* the knowledge and talents they *need* to address students' learning challenges. *Professional development* is not applicable unless it causes *teachers* to enrich their instruction or produces administrators who are respected, people-oriented school leaders.

To provide effective T.I.P.S., the principal and administrative team can provide professional development to the staff so they then can F.E.E.D. students in acquiring the necessary skills for development. This is another topic that can be deeply examined, but we will only touch on a few major points.

Professional development (PD) is a must for educators. It helps new teachers learn advanced techniques, seasoned teachers find new methods of making instruction exciting and rewarding, and top-chef teachers to renew and reenergize. The main goal is to improve staff skills and proficiencies needed to create increased educational attainment for students by creating new systems. However, according to Dr. Annette Simmons, who listed "Four Reasons Why Teachers Hate Professional Development" (August 2016), educators want the same thing their students do: "motivation, encouragement, support, and a general sense of excitement that injects and energetic and productive vibe into the classroom." She refers to PD as affectionately called "the day teachers don't teach but get sent to various places in the district to attend a day of supposed enrichment but usually ends up as a waste of time and I would have rather spent the day in my room catching up on my work" – a mouthful. PD must be relevant and worth the time of teachers, something that can be extended in the classroom and will make a transformation for students.

As a consultant who provides many PD sessions, I know what educators say is important when they are given this opportunity. First and foremost, please F.E.E.D. us (*If You Don't Feed the TEACHERS, They Eat the Students!* has many ideas). Drinks and snacks add so much to a day of PD.

Second, have it in a comfortable setting where we feel appreciated, can write and take notes on a table, have accessible restrooms, and snacks/water throughout the day. The personal needs must be met first before any learning and engagement will occur.

> **"**
> It is nice to be important but it is far more important to be nice.
> **Source unknown**
> **"**

Once we have sent the message to the attendees that you *do matter*, the following are additional components to consider:

✓ Have teachers involved in the planning of the session(s) so it relates to their needs. Have a team of teachers work with the consultant(s) presenting so the goals and outcomes are clear and concise.

✓ Plan ongoing PD so the presenter(s) can return throughout the year to answer questions, address concerns, demonstrate additional strategies, and just "check in."

> Student achievement at the end of the year is directly related to the degree to which the teacher establishes good control of the classroom procedures in the very first week of the school year.
>
> **Harry Wong**

✓ Don't have one PD fits all. If the topic is on "how to teach students to become effective note-takers," don't have teachers attend who would never teach or use this focus.

✓ Drive-through PD is not effective where everyone gathers so they can earn their credits, and it is useless for most – with a "FLASH and DASH" presenter.

✓ Make sure the presenter is well versed in the topic, the audience, the needs, the expected outcomes, and any additional information that will help her/him be prepared. An unprepared presenter can be a disaster.

✓ Include many activities where participants are encouraged to engage, respond, share, ask questions, and provide *feedback*.

✓ PD must be ongoing, sustained, classroom-focused, and research-based.

✓ Excellent PD also can F.E.E.D. the teachers with amazing results.

Michael Fullen believes "the purpose of staff development is not just to implement instructional innovations; its central purpose is to build strong collaborative work cultures that will develop the long term capacity for change." PD is effective only when planned by the staff, includes short- and long-term goals, and allows for successful implementation.

F.O.O.D (Fulfilling Opportunities Offered Daily) for Thought

The following provides specific activities and ideas that a school staff can implement:

• Look at the list of skills recommended for students. As a team, determine which skills you are including in your instruction, and how. Share the list with the entire staff.

> **"**
> Schooling is first and foremost about relationships between and among students and teachers, and . . . community building . . . [which improves] teaching and learning.
> **H. Thomas Sergiovanni**
> in *Building Community in Schools*
> **"**

- Develop mini workshops for students to teach them the essential skills.

- Develop a skill analysis overview to give to students (or find one online) and as a team review and discuss the abilities that are lacking.

- Have teams review the recommended goals of a successful school, discuss what is being accomplished, and make any changes or additions:

➢ Appreciate education and develop a joy for learning.

➢ Respect who they are – physically, intellectually, socially, and emotionally.

➢ Realize they are responsible for their own behavior and must deal with the consequences.

➢ Learn how to learn.

➢ Acquire a strong work ethic.

➢ Appreciate the importance of trying and succeeding – with failure sometimes in between.

➢ Develop a sense of honesty and integrity.

➢ Understand how to respect diversity, differences, and determination.

➢ Strive to set and accomplish goals.

➢ Learn from valuable and authentic feedback.

- Examine the skills for the workforce and determine where each skill is addressed within the curriculum. Begin analyzing this information.

- Purchase the book *The Four O'Clock Faculty; A Rogue Guide to Revolutionizing Professional Development* by Rich Czyz for the administrative team to read before planning PD. Share their findings with the staff.

- Scrutinize the reactions to feedback and determine how to respond to each one:

  a. Anger – "I've had enough of this."

  b. Denial – "I can't see any problem with that."

> That which we persist in doing becomes easier, not that the task itself has become easier, but that our ability to perform it has improved.
> **Ralph Waldo Emerson**

c. Blame – "It's not my fault" (what can you expect when the patient won't listen?).

d. Rationalize – "I've had a bad week. Doesn't everyone do this?"

e. Acceptance – "I see now."

f. Renewed action – "Let me rethink, restart, recreate, and redo."

- Ask teams to identify the attributes of extraordinary PD presentations.

- Request teams to determine PD needs and begin to develop team plans for future PD.

- Take each skill to be taught and work with small groups of students determining their strengths and areas of concern.

- Have students list one or two dreams. Work with them to turn their dreams into goals.

- Assign students simple jobs in the school and classroom to learn responsibility.

- Have the students develop *vision boards* that display their hopes and dreams for the future. Have them displayed throughout the school for everyone to view.

- Let students build *buddy benches* for the outside of the school where new students can sit to make friends. Have a buddy club of students who watch out for new, lonely, or detached students.

- Have students write a paragraph on "how they learn best," including the noise level, space, seating, and all variables. As a team reviews their entries and assesses them, they are given opportunities to meet with students to discuss their needs.

- Have the students begin to journal every day upon entering a designated class, possibly in the beginning of the day and at the end. Have them share when they feel comfortable.

After a great time with great service and feeling F.E.D., we can focus on a main ingredient for success, which is *fun*.

SIX ACTIONS

MY BEST TEACHERS DID TO F.E.E.D. ME

1. She taught will and she listened to all students' opinions.

2. I fell like I related to her.

3. She help me be accountable.

4. She incorporated all of her students.

5. She seemed passionate about the things she taught.

6. She never faked anything.

By | Hannah Burr, 10th grade

MENU

Juvenile or Parental Delinquency
"We read in the paper, we hear on the air of the
Killing and stealing and crime everywhere.
We sigh and we say, as we notice the trend,
This young generation, where will it all end?
But can we be sure it's their fault alone?
Too much money to spend, too much idle time;
Too many movies of passion and crime;
Too many books not fit to read;
Too many evils in what they hear;
Too many kids encouraged to roam
By too many parents who don't stay at home;
Youth don't make the movies;
They don't write the books
That paint the pictures of gangsters and crooks.
They don't make the liquor,
They don't run the bars,
They don't make the laws
And they don't make the cars.
They don't make the drugs that idle the brain.
It's all done by older folks, greedy for gain.
And how many cases we find that it's true,
The label "DELINQUENCY" fits older folks too!

by Dallas Brown

CHAPTER 10

Fun: An Environment That Everyone Enjoys

Create an Environment Where Students and Adults Enjoy School and Have Fun

At five-star restaurants, you can see the wait staff, the managers, the top chefs, and the team having fun. They respect one another, enjoy one another, and appreciate the talents of all. Fun is imperative at the workplace. It doesn't need to be all of the time but has to be embedded into the core of the mission, vision, values, and employees. I have worked at many restaurants that had an incredible and fun staff. I looked forward to going to work. But I have also worked at a restaurant that was not fun at all – not for long.

At five-star schools, you see people enjoying one another, their profession, and *especially* the students. I had a student last year say to me, "Dr. Connors, I hope you don't mind but I love you ALMOST as much as I love my mama." This was an 8th grade male. I soared home that day, my ego was so big. Also, a student said to me, "You know you're my hero." Oh my. What else is there in the world? I truly believe, no matter where you work, if you can't have fun at work – you are missing a big piece of life. All of his life my father talked about "the day I retire – the day I retire." The day he retired – all he talked about was "the good ole days." He hardly ever lived in the moment and missed out on some fun times.

The critical question is this: Is work supposed to be fun? Yes, because fun is a "fun-damentally" motivating phenomena that keeps employees coming back and enjoying their job. We spend 8–12 hours a day at work, which is equivalent to a third to half of our lives. It is true that we don't know what we've got until we lose it, but it's also true that we don't know what we've been missing until it arrives. Hopefully, FUN is a vital element in your actuality. I once read, "May you have enough happiness to make you sweet, enough trials to make you strong, enough sorrow to keep you human, enough hope to make you happy, and enough fun to make you enjoy each day with vigor, value, and vitality" (author unknown).

> Education is the path from cocky ignorance to miserable uncertainty.
> **Mark Twain**

Our students come to school to see their friends, engage in schoolwide activities, and hopefully have some fun during each day. Laughter is contagious, and many times I see my students laughing and I just start because I know they are enjoying the moment. Our students need:

- Adults who care

- Positive discipline, not punishment

- To be involved

- Choice

- Engagement

- Empowerment

- Celebrations

- Laughter

Students also say so many funny things, like a recent 8th grade male who squawked out in class about 2:40 (20 minutes before the end of the day) – "Dr. Connors, is there any way you can give me a physical before 3:30 so I can try out for the softball team?" I'm not that kind of doctor. Or the student who said, "You weren't here yesterday. Did you get suspended?" You have to laugh. I come home every day with at least three or more situations that happened or comments said to me that make me love my job and the students even more.

Teaching is fun. If you aren't having fun, your students probably aren't, either. Mr. Ford, a member of my team, is always throwing a joke or funny comment into his math lesson. The kids *love* him and are constantly stopping by just to say "hey." His humor increases students' attention, motivation, excitement, interactions, and engagement. It also lessens anxiety and stress and "humanizes" him. Laughter is infectious – like yawning, it brings people together. Mr. Ford is the best who epitomizes everything a top-chef teacher does. He wins "teacher of the month" almost every month and ultimately teacher of the year.

Not all classwork or school activities need to be a game or a good time, but students who see school as a place where they can have FUN are more likely to pay attention, become motivated, and see learning as a tool to become

> Every child is gifted. They just unwrap their packages at different times.
> **Source unknown**

a success for life. Adding fun activities into your day can help engage students, especially those who struggle. Also, ensure the classroom is a friendly, welcoming, and inviting environment where ALL students can feel safe and nurtured. A fun atmosphere is one where diversity is celebrated and we find GOLD in every student. Sometimes, we have to "dig through a lot of dirt to find the gold," but we know it is there and we just keep digging. Years ago I asked a group of students at varying ages what they wanted from teachers. Their responses included:

> Even if a student's life away from school is bleak and miserable, she/he will work if what she/he finds in school is satisfying.
> **William Glasser**

- Smile.

- Greet me each day and say my name.

- Give me attention and make me feel valued.

- Show me.

- Engage me.

- Notice me and if I have a new shirt or haircut.

- Trust me.

- Empower me.

- Ask about me.

- Let me have time to think, enjoy, explore, and laugh!

Humor must be authentic – not forced. When I was observing student teachers years ago, I had one of them call me the night before his observation. He said, "I'm just checking to make sure you will observe me tomorrow." "Yes," I said. "Any special activity going on?" He responded, "You must be there tomorrow, because I plan to be *funny,* and I don't want you to miss it." He totally missed the point but did a great job, and indeed integrated humor into his classroom. He is still teaching to this day. Especially, don't mistake sarcasm for humor. Students don't like to feel humiliated or demeaned. James Gordon, a professor at Brigham Young University, says, "When students are having fun, the class time virtually flies by, and the 50 minutes of class seem like a mere 48." The happiest of people don't necessarily have the best of everything; they just make the most of everything that comes along their way.

One of my favorite quotes is "We don't stop playing because we're old, we're old because we've stopped playing" (author unknown). Unfortunately, there are a few educators who have stopped playing and have lost enthusiasm for their job and make excuses for their lack of commitment. Not *top-chef teachers*; they are excited,

> You wouldn't worry so much about what other people thought if you realized how seldom they do.
> **Eleanor Roosevelt**

> The best kind of friend is the kind you can sit on a porch and swing with, never say a word, and then walk away feeling like it was the best conversation you've ever had.
> **Author unknown**

energized, and student-focused who go above and beyond the required expectations. Even with all of the challenges of today, these special teachers and administrators F.E.E.D. students regularly with a NEVER GIVE UP and winning attitude. How? Just as the quote implies – they never stop playing and having fun. Play, you say? In school? What does that really mean?

The word *play* has many definitions. My favorite is "to move freely within limits, to amuse yourself and have fun." Top-chef teachers enjoy the students and focus on having fabulous days most of the time. They realize that one recipe does not meet the needs of every students. Consequently, they continuously look for each student's gifts to capitalize on and turn them into teachable moments. They don't ask why; they ask how. Overall, they PLAY, as follows:

P-repare for each day, lesson, and student. They encourage students to develop their own individual plan for learning and celebrate their success. These top-chef teachers have determination and intellectual discipline along with high anticipations for all.

L-earn along with students. The best teachers never forget what it is like to be a student and the best administrators never forget what it is to be a teacher. To encourage life-long the love of learning, we must model it to *engage* and *empower* students.

A-djust the lessons and their attitude when necessary. Teachers who *play* realize that there will be disruptions and distractions during the day. These top-chef teachers go with the flow and don't lose control over that which can't be controlled. They also maintain a positive attitude and communicate their attitude by how they spend their time modeling effectiveness, learning about every student, respond to disruptions rather than react, and look at ways to reward students doing the right thing.

Y-earn for success for all. The top-chef teachers realize that they are there for every student – not just the best and brightest. You can't have the motto "teach the best – forget the rest." These teachers serve as advocates for the students.

To *play,* one must be in a student-centered school where the missions and vision are developed, practiced, and espoused by all. This can be accomplished in schools where the leadership recognizes the importance of the schoolwide team first and then empowers individual teams. Remember to play. Enjoy your life, profession, colleagues, and especially students. As Wayne Dyer said, "Never let an old person enter your body" and be "forever young."

No one ever went to their deathbed saying, "You know, I wish I had eaten more rice cakes."
Amy Krouse Rosenthal

We all need our needs basic needs met. We are driven by our need to survive. We need to feel a sense of *belonging* and of being *loved*. We need knowledge and skill to gain *power* so that we can gain control of our own lives. We need to feel *free* to be who we are. And we must bring joy and *fun* into our lives. With all the pressures of testing, struggles, new programs, assessment, and teacher evaluations – DO NOT allow the fun to leave schools. And never forget what we learned from Noah.

Lessons We Learned from Noah (source unknown):

1. Don't miss the boat.

2. Remember – we are ALL in the same boat.

3. Plan ahead. It wasn't raining when Noah built the boat.

4. Stay fit. When you are 600 years old, someone may ask you to do something really BIG!

5. Don't listen to critics.; just get on with the job that needs to be done.

6. Build your future on high ground.

7. For safety's sake – travel in pairs.

8. Speed isn't always an advantage. The snails were on board with the cheetahs.

9. When you are stressed – float a while.

10. Remember – the ark was built by amateurs – the *Titanic* by professionals.

11. No matter the storm – there is always a RAINBOW waiting.

Bon apétit!

F.O.O.D (Fulfilling Opportunities Offered Daily) for Thought

The following are specific ideas and activities to discuss and implement as a staff:

- Have staff determine a time each week where they will meet as a team to discuss something they can do together with students that renews and reenergizes everyone.

- Have the staff all determine their *bucket list,* and throughout the beginning meetings of the year each staff member gives a three-to-five-minute presentation on what they want to experience in their life.

- Encourage the staff to think of three to five great things that happened that day *before* you close your eyes to sleep. Focus on what you *did* – not failures. You will sleep more peacefully.

- Go to the website http://www.questforhumor.com to peruse materials on humor.

- Establish professional and personal rituals that include fun, students, and colleagues.

- Try to think of something funny to say to a colleague. Try to do five different "funnies" for a week to five different colleagues.

- Make sure you smile. When students are asked what they want from their teachers, many said, "I just wish she/he would smile."

- Discuss the funny things your students have said or written (word problem: Joanna works in an office. Her computer is a standalone system. What is a standalone computer system? Student's answer: It doesn't come with a chair.).

- Find some humorous YouTube videos and show short ones at staff meetings.

- When possible, make staff meetings *fun.* Have a different team plan a short fun activity for each meeting. A little competition can be healthy when teams begin to try to prepare for a better meeting. When you have a district/state mandate that you must go over, ask some staff to help you make it less boring. And of course, *always have food* at staff meetings.

- Ask students to develop a list of the characteristics of the best teachers. Share and discuss.

When everything is said and done and we have had a five-star experience, we must reflect on all of the ingredients. Reflection is a time to consolidate and express your thinking.

FIVE ACTIONS

MY BEST TEACHERS DID TO F.E.E.D. ME

1. Mrs. Baulkman: encouraged me to do better.

2. Mr. Quatamon: did projects and gave ideas to me to study and learn my subjects within school.

3. Mrs. Porter: everything I didn't understand in class she would not move on to the next subject.

4. Mrs. Harrison: kept putting me out there to step out of my comfort zone and go out and do more things.

5. My teachers made me a leader making me feel like I got this and I know exactly what I'm doing.

By | Merrie Gordon, 9th grade

A sign I have in my classroom (source unknown):

Dear Students,
I know when you're texting in class.
Seriously, no one just looks down at their crotch and smiles.
Sincerely, Your Teacher.

Ten ways to neutralize your nemesis:

1. Analyze your role in the conflict.

2. Laugh away an insult.

3. Avoid public confrontation.

4. ALWAYS question the question.

5. Kill with kindness and tact.

6. Seek first to understand and then think about the situation.

7. Build up your E.A.G.L.E.S. to outnumber the D.U.C.K.S. and confront the D.U.C.K.S. with respect.

8. Stay visible – do not retreat.

9. Be real – love yourself and do not give in to negativity.

10. Develop positive networks and support groups to reflect and laugh.

> Always put yourself in others' shoes. If you feel that it hurts you, it probably hurts the other person too.
>
> **Author unknown**

> We don't get burned out because of what we do. We get burned out because we forget WHY WE DO IT!
>
> **Neila A. Connors**

Does this program motivate students?

NEVER GIVE UP!

Source unknown

CHAPTER 11

"Check, Please": Reflection Shows the Experience Was Worth It

Reflection on Empowering Teachers to F.E.E.D. Students so They Don't S.T.A.R.V.E

After a fabulous experience at a five-star restaurant, it is fun to reflect on the experience. We talk about the meal, the service, our favorite part of the event, and anything else to determine it was truly worth it. I have friends that like to visit new restaurants in our area. I always call them the next day to find out if I will be going to the restaurant. We talk about ambiance, cost, food, service, the facilities, and anything else that arises. At the end of our conversation, I always know if it is a restaurant worth trying. Reflection is a check-up from the neck-up.

Five-star schools have top-chef teachers that at the beginning of a new school year realize the importance of the first day and week determining the rest of the year. During that first week, month, and throughout the year they *reflect, renew,* and *reenergize.* They take a serious look at their life, their profession, and their commitment to being the best.

As they *reflect,* they ask the following questions:

○ What successes did I experience last year, and how can I capitalize on them on a continual basis?

○ Did I ensure success for ALL of my students?

○ How effective am I in being a positive schoolwide team member?

○ Do I help spread the mission and philosophy of the school?

○ Do I attempt to maintain a positive attitude as much as possible?

○ Am I supportive of team members and colleagues needing a "shoulder to cry/rest on"?

○ Do I let the important people in my life know they are so important?

○ Do I maintain a connection to as many parents/guardians as possible?

○ Do I maintain a sense of humor and laugh at least once a day (fake it until you make it)?

○ Do I live each day to the fullest focusing on successes and highlights?

As you *renew,* ask these questions:

○ Why do I teach?

○ What can I do to improve personally and professionally?

○ How can I connect with more students?

○ How can I involve more parents?

○ What can I do to be a better team member and more supportive of my principal, administrative team, and colleagues?

○ What new and innovative strategies do I look forward to trying?

○ What risks will I take?

○ What will I continue to do to remain updated concerning new trends, research, and techniques?

○ How can I live each day to the fullest by living, loving, learning, and laughing?

And as you *reenergize,* take time to involve yourself in the following activities:

○ Call someone you haven't spoken to in a long time and let them know about your love of teaching and students.

○ Spend an entire day engaged in something you love doing but haven't done in a long time.

○ Make a special date with your "significant other," include some surprises, and only talk for 15 minutes about work.

○ Call a friend and go to a movie or lunch.

○ Take the time to journal and write an overview of your career in education, including names of students that you have "touched."

○ Play some of your favorite songs loud and dance through your house – include pets and family members.

○ Call a parent, relative, and/or friend and tell them how special they are to you.

- ○ Read at least one fictional novel.

- ○ Take a day to volunteer at a homeless shelter, hospital, or boys and girls club.

- ○ **Remember WHY you became and educator.**

As you *reflect, renew, and reenergize*, think honestly about each response. Remember, teaching is the most difficult profession in existence. It is so important that you remember that teaching is not a popularity contest and you must continue to realize without YOU – we wouldn't have all the other professions. You make a difference on a daily basis and there are students that have a successful life and career because of YOU!

Five-star schools also see the need for students reflecting on their learning, their goals, and overall thoughts. I think it is so sad that in many schools, at the end of the day a bell may ring or the students just know the day is done and they rush out of the building with no closure to the day. Reflection is about becoming aware of your own thinking processes, and being able to make those transparent to others. In *Clarity in the Classroom* (2010), Michael Absolum wrote, "Reflection captures the idea that if a gap is found between how we would want teaching and learning to be and how it actually is, then something will be done to close that gap; it is not enough just to reflect or identify that there is a gap." Teachers themselves can become reflective practitioners who reflect with their students on the teaching and learning process, and teach their students to use reflective strategies to strengthen their own capacity to learn.

In my dream school, we would leave the last 10–15 minutes for students to verbally reflect or write in their journals (which I am a big believer in) about their day's pluses and minuses. I would want them to respond to the following questions:

- • How was your day?

- • What was something special about today?

- • What was a kind endeavor you engaged in?

- • Did someone do something nice for you today?

- • What were three things you learned?

- • Do you have any homework and do you have everything you need to complete it at home?

Reflection is one of the many "R's" needed to F.E.E.D. students along with relationships, respect, relevance, rigor, reinforcement, and recognition. Reflection would also occur at the end of every class. It is about becoming aware of your own thinking advancements and being able to share with others. Teachers become reflective specialists who reveal with their students the necessary strategies to enhance the teaching/learning processes.

> I don't want to be an *icon*, I want to be an *inspiration*.
>
> **Tyler Perry**

Reflection is a valuable tool to get students to think about their thinking – metacognition.

We can use the tools of journaling, group discussions, informal conversations, interviews, blogs, surveys, questionnaires, and many more to provide a reflective platform. Just like we reflected on our dining experience, wouldn't it be valuable if students reflected and spoke about their day and experiences before exiting the school? When I do this, there is a more composed exit to the day. Reflection ROCKS!

Students need successful experiences, to be involved, immediate feedback, and time for reflection. During summer school, my students had so many valuable and current reflections of today's government, schooling, family situations, and racism. I was impressed with their knowledge base and deep thinking. We don't take the time in schools to have those kind of conversations because stressed teachers are so concerned with getting through the curriculum and preparing for the end of the year tests. And you can't blame them – it's the priority of the state and district and unfortunate. As I have stressed throughout this "cookbook" – the number one priority in schools must be *relationships* along with *connections*. Compassionate teachers are viewed as relationship coaches and the *guide on the side* versus the *sage on the stage*. The relationships we develop set the tone and disposition of our school and classrooms.

A daily reflection for growth is a foremost element of the learning process. We are reflective humans and our minds are always spinning. We need to teach our students the value of reflection and how it contributes to development and advancement. As Starr Sackstein stated in an article titled "Deeper Reflection, Deeper Learning," student reflections can be the thing to really change the way we understand student learning. As we empower students to share their ideas about how and what they have taken away from different learning experiences, we gain a deeper knowledge of our practice and how to improve both instruction and feedback for every child. Once students have begun to reflect regularly, the level of their work naturally develops with practice.

The growth mindset viewpoint indicates that working hard involves thinking hard, which involves reflecting on and changing our strategies so we become more and more effective learners over time.

The growth mindset philosophy emphasizes reflection where students have a desire to learn while embracing challenges, endurances, recognizes efforts, learns from criticism, and finds lessons and inspirations in the success of others. Go to the website: http://www.edutopia.org/article/growth-mindset-resources, where a plethora of tools and videos showing the importance of this philosophy are available. You learn it is a driving philosophy and not just a tool. Staff also need to embrace reflection and keep a reflective journal where they document learnings, recipes that don't work, thoughts for the day, great things that happened, and hopes and dreams. Developing reflective lesson plans is also an effective process to get students thinking.

Starr Sackstein concluded her article:

After I do my reflections, I always make sure to develop an action plan. It's not enough to think about how things went or just to question, I have to try to change what I am doing for the better. This takes a deliberate effort and finding the right strategies to grow. Reflection is a huge part of my educational diet, and it has made me a better person, mother, and educator; and now as a leaders, I try to model and share reflective practices with the team that I am a part of so we can all grow together.

F.O.O.D (Fulfilling Opportunities Offered Daily) for Thought

In conclusion, I would like to reflect on some major ingredients stressed throughout this cookbook as recipes for success:

- When developing a discipline plan, include a "Better Choices Sheet" as created by Amie Dean. The student must complete the following:

Name _____ Date _____ Name _____

My actions were as follows: (What I Did) _____

_____

A better choice, which I will do next time is: _____

_____

Why I made the bad choice: _____

_____

To help myself, the next time something like this happens, I will _____

Student Signature: _____

Teacher/Team: _____

- In planning lessons, ask yourself: Are my lessons culturally responsive? Do they take into consideration all of the learners in my classroom? Include reflective thinking? Involve students?

- Know your purpose. If unsure or having a rough day, place your hand over your heart. Feel that beating heart? It's called PURPOSE. You are alive for a reason; don't ever give up.

- Parents are an essential element to F.E.E.D. students. Interact, engage, involve, and appreciate the parent connection. Go to the website www.partnershipschools.org for specific ideas and activities.

- Reflect on a lesson you taught describing what went well, what didn't, and how you could enrich the lesson and/or make it better.

As you go through your daily lessons and activities, remember the importance of reflection.

Teach student to reflect through journaling, speaking, presentations, and group work. Take the time to review your "menu" each day to ensure it is nourishing, enticing, engaging, and delicious. Good luck in becoming a five-star school with top-chef teachers who F.E.E.D. students so they don't S.T.A.R.V.E. *Bon appétit!*

Confucius on Wisdom

- By reflection – the noblest
- By imitation – the easiest
- By experience – the bitterest

When you need a break, take a MINI-VACATION by:

✓ Hurry slowly and sing

✓ Ponder and love

✓ Doodle

✓ Laugh

✓ Share

✓ Take a walk

✓ Dream

✓ Pet a dog or cat or something . . .

✓ Just BE

✓ Breathe

✓ Celebrate the little moments

✓ SMILE

Neila A. Connors

"
You laugh, you cry, and you work harder than you ever thought you could.
    Some days you're trying to change the world and some days you're just trying to make it through the day.
    Your wallet is empty, your *heart* is full and your *mind* is packed with memories of students who have changed your life.
    Just another day as an extraordinary EDUCATOR!

Author unknown
"

"
Yesterday is history, tomorrow is a mystery, and today is a gift. That's why it's called the present.

Author unknown
"

10 Signs of a Positive Workplace

By Linnda Durre, PhD, Monster Contributing Writer

As a business consultant, corporate trainer, and psychotherapist for many years, many people have asked me, "How can I cope with negativity at work? Are there good organizations to work for? How can I spot one and get hired?"

(continued)

Positive workplaces tend to exhibit a common set of traits that foster excellence, productivity, and camaraderie. Here are 10 characteristics of a healthy workplace to look for:

1. Positive Values

   A positive mission statement outlines the goals and demonstrative behavior that exemplify the highest commitment to quality and service to each other, the company, customers, and shareholders. The company sets out to achieve Its goals in ethical, honest ways with an elevated sense of purpose to improving the planet and humanity.

2. Relaxed and Productive Atmosphere

   People enjoy coming to work and feel appreciated, acknowledged, and rewarded. Signs of fear, bullying, harassment, and intimidation are absent. Creativity, productivity, and thinking outside the box flourish.

3. Commitment to Excellence

   Employees give 200%. They strive to be the best and to deliver top-quality services. They take responsibility for their actions and decisions.

4. Open and Honest Communication

   Everyone communicates in a cards-on-the-table manner solving difficulties in a positive way. They don't play nasty revenge games when given difficult feedback. Instead, they view feedback as an opportunity for growth.

5. Cooperation, Support, and Empowerment

   Can-do, go-the-extra-mile, and win–win attitudes are evident. Employees have a sense of camaraderie, cooperation, and empowerment. Healthy competition exists without vengeful, spiteful backstabbing.

6. Sense of Humor

   Employees keep things in perspective, have fun, and laugh. Laughter generates endorphins, our natural antidepressants.

7. Compassion, Respect, and Understanding

   Kindness and understanding prevail when employees face challenges such as accidents illnesses, personal tragedies, and natural disasters. People will usually go the extra mile for others when they're treated well and with understanding, compassion, and respect.

8. **Flexibility**

   The company and its employees embrace change, accommodate new trends and technology, and incorporate new skills. They know if they don't, the business will end up a dinosaur. As the saying goes, "Change is the only constant."

9. **Positive Reinforcement**

   People need acknowledgment, appreciation, and gratitude to be motivated. Genuine compliments, rewards, bonuses, raises, promotions, and certificates of achievement are oil in the machinery. The company thanks employees regularly in these ways.

10. **Emphasis on Health, Family, and Environment**

    The organization offers comprehensive health insurance with weight loss, and substance-abuse programs. The organization is environmentally aware by encouraging solar power and recycling.

Traits and Skills Required for Excellence in Teaching by Neila A. Connors

- *Demonstrates enthusiasm and a zest for living with passion*
- *Has a sense of humor*
- *Shows a love of teaching and subject matter*
- *Displays the ability to organize and schedule time appropriately*

(continued)

- *Maintains positive discipline—fair but firm with dignity and respect*

- *Demonstrates a love and understanding of students, diversity, lifestyle choices, and achievement*

- *Shows a cooperative spirit and is a team player*

- *Displays a personal and professional attitude and team spirit*

- *Recognizes and provides for individual differences and learning styles*

- *Demonstrates an effective use of available materials, resources, and technology*

- *Has a willingness to accept constructive criticism*

- *Uses great judgment in dealing with behavior issues and teaches students expectations*

- *Has a pleasing personality, people skills, and a positive attitude*

- *Is skilled in communication with colleagues, team members, students, parents, and has effective people skills*

- *Displays genuine interest in all students and celebrates diversity*

- *Uses common sense and good judgment*

- *Demonstrates patience and tolerance for all walks of life*

- *Is dependable and loyal to the school, students, and community*

- *Creates a pleasant and attractive classroom atmosphere conducive to learning, success, and all students*

- *Uses a variety of motivational techniques and methods and is receptive to new ideas*

- *Stimulates students to reflect, creatively think, and problem-solve*

- *Handles routine procedures*

- *Is the student advocate who goes above and beyond to help all students succeed*

- *Is positive about change*

- *Invites parents to be a part of the learning/growing process of their children*

- *Has a fulfilled life outside of school and takes care of her/himself physically, intellectually, socially, emotionally, financially, and spiritually,*

- *Demonstrates self-discipline and has the ability to have FUN*

How Do You Rate?

Bloom's Taxonomy

Knowledge	the remembering of learned material
Comprehension	the grasping of meaning
Application	using learned material in new situations
Analysis	understanding the relationships between parts and the organizational structure
Synthesis	putting parts together to form a new whole
Evaluation	judging value

Effective Strategies to Engage All Families

Create a family resource center:

–in-school with parent volunteers

–Connect with community centers/leaders

–Partner with community businesses

–area with specific school information

Life is Precious, and So Are You
NEILA A. CONNORS

*Your life is what YOU make it, based
on the attitude you choose.*

*The way YOU deal with EVERY day, tells
if you win or lose.*

*To win you must be
thoughtful, and love all that
YOU ARE.*

*Appreciate YOUR talents,
shoot for YOUR shining star.*

*Eat well, sleep sound, and
exercise, begin each day with
prayer.*

*Set your course by setting goals,
take risks and learn to care.*

*Smile, love, give lots of hugs,
respect the human race.*

*Don't criticize, complain, or
whine, maintain a growing pace.*

*Words like "wish" and "should" and
"can't" must NEVER cross your tongue.*

*Go for the gold—stretch and try,
leave no song unsung.*

*For life's too short to waste a
day, or live without a plan.*

*So THINK and DREAM, don't give
up, and*

ALWAYS say "I CAN!"

**Hugs, and HERE's CHEERS
to a FABULOUS LIFE and
PROFESSION! Be kind and
take care of YOU!**

Neila